Fishing Yellowstone
Hatches

Craig Mathews

Fishing Yellowstone Hatches

by
JOHN JURACEK
and
CRAIG MATHEWS

First Published 1992 by
Blue Ribbon Flies
West Yellowstone, MT 59758
Printed in U.S.A.

Contents

Acknowledgments

The accumulation of information on insect hatches is a time consuming process, and we have been fortunate to have good friends help us along the way. Thanks go to Gary Blackburn, Paul Brown, the late Bob Hoar, Nick Nicklas, Dave Schultz, and Tom Young for bringing us insect samples and always keeping a sharp eye on what's happening on the water.

Special thanks go to Paul Brown, Verlyn Klinkenborg, and Tom Young for their valuable comments and criticisms on the text.

We owe a special debt of gratitude to entomologist Daniel Gustafson, Ph.D., for always taking time to visit with us and look at our collections. Besides making numerous species identifications and verifying others, he too read the text and set us straight on many entomological matters.

We wish to thank Tracy Ikard, computer wizard, for rescuing us repeatedly when we encountered computer problems.

Thanks also to Jackie Mathews for assistance in making corrections to the text, and to Ken Takata for taking the cover photographs.

Introduction

An old fly fishing friend of ours, one with many years of experience, once commented to us that he has never paid attention to insect hatches and never would as long as he continued to fish. He boasted that he could catch trout on any river, anytime, without paying mind to any insects that might be around. Yes, we had to agree, he probably could. Many other fishermen can too. But that attitude struck us, and still does, as particularly odd for a fly fisherman.

It seems only natural that fly fishermen should be curious about insect hatches, and not just because a knowledge of them can improve angling success, which it most certainly does. More importantly, we should take an interest in insects because they are, after all, the root of our sport. Without them there is no basis for fly fishing.

The Yellowstone area has a long history of superb fly fishing for trout. Excellent aquatic insect populations are one factor that has contributed mightily to this fishing. An incredible wealth and diversity of aquatic insects thrive in the lakes and rivers here, and it is possible to find fish feeding on insects every day of the season.

There is surprisingly little information available on the insect hatches of this area in published fly fishing books. Much of what does exist is included in books which cover the entire country. By necessity the information contained in them is brief, and often of little value to fishermen concentrating on one area. Also, some hatches simply haven't been known well enough to have been written about.

In *Fishing Yellowstone Hatches* we've attempted to describe the important hatches of this area, based on our experiences and those of friends. In an area as vast as Yellowstone it would take several lifetimes to assemble a complete list of all the hatches. We feel our list is a worthwhile beginning, all the while acknowledging its shortcomings.

Because the Yellowstone region is so large, it is important to note what area we have covered. We include all of Yellowstone Park. West of Yellowstone Park we include the area from Henry's Fork of the Snake in Idaho north to Ennis, Montana. The Gallatin River drainage is included on the north to the point where the Gallatin River leaves Gallatin Canyon. Many of the hatches we write about occur over a much larger area, and the information we give (except, perhaps, the emergence dates) should be found useful outside the boundaries we mention. Even within our geographic area, many of these insect hatches are more widespread than our lists may indicate. We aren't able to mention all the waters a specific hatch may occur on, just the most important ones.

The emergence dates we provide are based on information from early, late, and normal seasons. Though we feel they are extremely accurate, the dates should probably still be viewed as guidelines. The species are covered in the order they appear during the season.

One note on insect names. If an insect has a commonly accepted name we have used it. If it does not (this pertains mostly to caddisflies, and reflects how poorly they are understood) we have used their real name, and yes, they're Latin. Many fishermen feel using Latin names is somehow akin to snobbery, but this isn't true. Since we have to call them something, and because it's just as easy to say *Hydropsyche* as it is to say "it was that caddis with tan wings and a brownish body in about a size #14 or #16," we have taken the Latin route when necessary.

Finally, when we talk about the Madison River it should be assumed we mean the water below Quake Lake, unless otherwise noted.

Mayflies

Mayflies can be found emerging every month of the year in the Yellowstone area. They are particularly abundant from May through October and are an important food source for trout during this time period. Mayflies are responsible for many of the great fly fishing opportunities that arise during the season, and a knowledge of their habits is invaluable for an angler.

Mayflies inhabit every trout stream and the number of species a stream can hold is often amazing. Our friend Dan Gustafson has found over sixty species on the Gallatin River alone, a sign of remarkable diversity in habitat. Of course not all rivers support so many species, and not all species are important to fly fishermen. Some mayflies are not abundant enough to warrant individual concern, while other species are so closely related in behavior that they can be considered synonymous by fishermen. Other mayflies are simply not available to trout in quantities large enough to require any attention from fishermen.

The species we discuss are responsible for virtually all of a Yellowstone angler's mayfly fishing. The list is actually quite short, and if you do not fish certain rivers or at certain times of the year, the list shrinks even more.

While each species has its own peculiarities, most demonstrate a preference for similar emergence and egglaying conditions. Knowing when the best mayfly activity will occur is as important as knowing the individual traits of a given species.

The heaviest mayfly emergences generally take place in overcast, cool weather. Misting rain or snow showers are ideal and stir the blood of all fly fishermen aware of this fact.

Though we can find no substantiation for this theory among professional entomologists, every experienced angler we know is in agreement on this point. Entomologists tell us that mayflies may actually prefer warm, dry conditions, and that they hatch just as abundantly on those kinds of days. We've been told cool weather simply concentrates the emergence over a short time period, and that during warm, dry days just as many mayflies emerge but do so by trickling off over longer periods.

We have trouble accepting that theory because it runs counter to years of observation by so many people. While inclement weather is not a strict requirement for good hatches (we have all seen great emergences on nice days), there is no doubt in our minds that many more flies come off when the weather is bad.

Of one thing we *are* sure: the best *fishing* during mayfly hatches is definitely on days when the weather is poor. If not because there are more mayflies, then certainly because they ride the water longer in cool weather, and suffer more emergence defects. Both these factors give the fish a better chance to feed on them. Too, trout in general (and browns specifically) seem to feel more comfortable feeding under overcast skies. This makes approaching and casting to them easier.

Of the mayfly spinners important to fishermen, all need moderately warm, calm conditions to lay their eggs. Wind stronger than a slight breeze, cold temperatures, or any precipitation precludes the spinners from reaching the water.

Attention to the weather then, as well as learning the habits of the prevailing mayflies, can be very important to successfully fishing Yellowstone mayfly activity.

Baetis tricaudatus

The fishing season has fully arrived when the first of these mayflies are seen drifting the currents of the Madison River. Their emergences herald the arrival of spring, along with the migrating antelope and newly hatched goslings that frequent the river bottom below Quake Lake. Runoff is still several weeks away, and the trout feed steadily on the tiny duns in the low, clear water.

We always feel a sense of relief knowing that the mayflies and the trout (not to mention ourselves) have survived another Montana winter. We have endured almost seven months waiting for these May days, and we always have a box full of new fly patterns to try.

Baetis tricaudatus (Bee'-tiss try-caw-day'-tuss) is one of two *Baetis* species found here that are important to fishermen. The other is *Baetis punctiventris*, which is covered in the following chapter. *Baetis tricaudatus* inhabits every trout stream in the Yellowstone area and is often the most abundant mayfly in a given stream. Depending on the river, emergences can occur during any month, but typically there are two peaks: May through June, and September through October. *Baetis* are small mayflies, but their emergences are usually so concentrated that even large fish can feed efficiently on them.

There is extensive variation in the appearance and size of *B. tricaudatus*, depending on the river and the time of year they emerge. Their size can run from #16 to #24, an exceptional range exhibited by no other mayfly in the area. Body color of the nymphs and duns varies from cream to olive to gray to brown, as well as all shades in between. Even within a given emergence there can be considerable variation in color (and occasionally size).

But there are some common features among *Baetis tricaudatus*. The nymphs all have the same streamlined body shape and three tails. They are superb swimmers, and move quickly through the water in short, rapid bursts.

Baetis tricaudatus duns have two tails, slender bodies, and tiny hind wings. The hind wings are so tiny in fact, that they are usually visible only with magnification.

The spinners of *B. tricaudatus* are rarely seen and their fate is somewhat unclear. We know that at least one strategy the females use for egglaying is to crawl under the water on rocks, logs, etc. to deposit their eggs. While we have caught fish while blind fishing with wet spinner imitations, we have never encountered a situation where they were required. The spinners have clear wings, two tails, and body colors ranging from brown to an opaque gray.

Emergences of *Baetis tricaudatus* generally take place in afternoon; 1:00 p.m. to 4:00 p.m. is the usual time frame. Weather plays a big role in determining the length and intensity of an emergence. The heaviest emergences occur in cool, overcast conditions. Light rain or snow, common here in the spring and fall, almost guarantee a good hatch. Look for short, sporadic hatches when the weather is sunny and warm.

Baetis duns emerge from their nymphal shucks at the surface. During a sparse emergence, trout will sometimes feed on the fully emerged duns, but it is more common to find them taking nymphs and crippled duns in the surface film. In a heavy emergence, the fish will concentrate almost exclusively on the nymphs, porpoising and tailing as they pick off the nymphs just before they reach the surface film.

Though trout, especially the larger fish, prefer nymphs, it is not always necessary to use a nymph pattern. On the Firehole, Madison, Yellowstone, and Slough Creek in Yellowstone Park, trout will take dun and emerging dun patterns readily. On the Henry's Fork and Madison below Quake Lake, the largest fish invariably must be taken with nymph patterns. Smaller fish on these rivers will take adult patterns, but the big ones rarely sip even a natural dun from the surface.

Our tactics on the Madison and Gallatin, because of their pocketwater nature, are different than those we use on the other rivers. On the Madison and Gallatin we approach rising fish from directly below them. We often wade within fifteen feet of the fish, both to eliminate as many currents as possible between us and the fish, which reduces drag, and to improve our casting accuracy. During heavy emergences, which are common with *Baetis*, trout lock tightly into narrow feeding lanes. Getting close to the fish helps us consistently cast our flies in these narrow lanes. Then too, the wind usually blows stiffly during a *Baetis* emergence, and a close approach helps defeat the effect of wind on our casts.

If we are using a floating fly, such as a Sparkle Dun, it is much easier to see if the cast is kept short. When nymph fishing to trout rolling in the current seams, short upstream casts help us manage the inevitable drag that quickly takes over in so many pockets. We use unweighted nymphs, so they drift in the film at the same level the trout are feeding at. Sometimes we see the take as a fish rolls over the fly; other times the line simply goes taut.

Oddly enough, with a tiny *Baetis* nymph it is not always necessary to strike quickly when a fish takes. If a trout takes your fly and hooks himself, he will often continue feeding as long as you apply no pressure to him. We have waited a full minute before pressuring a fish that took our nymph, all the while watching him feed as if nothing had happened.

On rivers like the Firehole, Yellowstone, Slough Creek or the Henry's Fork, we approach the fish from the side and slightly upstream. These rivers don't allow you to get quite as close to the fish as, say, on the Madison. This, plus intricate surface currents, make drag a major problem, and it is best handled by casting across and downstream to the fish.

Baetis tricaudatus emergences can be extremely heavy, so much so that it is often difficult to compete with the naturals. You can do everything right, and still not catch fish, simply because of the competition your fly faces. It is important to single out one trout and concentrate on him; flock shooting, while tempting, is usually a fruitless tactic. It can also help to make short, quick presentations. That is, try to put your fly a foot above the trout and not let it drift more than a foot or two past him if he does not take. Short, accurate drifts, repeated quickly, increase the chance that your fly will be selected.

The fly patterns we fish with reflect the trout's preference for nymphs and impaired duns. Pheasant Tail nymphs, Sparkle Duns, *Baetis* Emergers, and Biplanes are among our favorite patterns. As we noted earlier, *Baetis* exhibit considerable variation in size. Much of this variation is seasonal, and our fly size changes accordingly. Spring *Baetis* emergences contain the largest individuals; size #16 is possible, but most will be size #18 and #20. Fall emergences contain individuals that range from size #20 to #24. Our most commonly used fly size is #18 in the spring, in the fall #22.

Despite the wide color range of the naturals, we tie our imitations (except the Pheasant Tail) with only grayish-olive bodies. We do not consider the body color to be a critical factor in the success of a given *Baetis* pattern, and a grayish-olive is representative of many of our *Baetis* populations.

Selected emergences:
    Firehole: April 10 - July 4, September 1 - November 7
    Madison (YNP): April 10 - July 8
    Madison: May 1 - June 7, September 1 - October 10
    Henry's Fork: April - November
    Yellowstone: August - October
    Slough Creek: July - October
    Gallatin: May - October

Baetis
punctiventris

Late October of last year was particularly brutal in Yellowstone. Heavy snows and temperatures as cold as thirty five below zero squelched our fishing season, and Yellowstone Park was forced to close on October twenty-second. The Park reopened briefly a few days later as conditions improved, and we made tracks for the Firehole River that same day.

We passed a few diehard anglers casting large streamers on the Madison for spawning browns, but we were after one last day of dry fly fishing before the Park closed for the season. As we left Madison Junction and climbed towards the Firehole, light snow began falling. As happens so often in the fall, a gusty breeze accompanied the snow. When we turned onto Fountain Flat drive, we began thinking a duck hunt on Hebgen Lake might have been a better idea. Snow was whipping across the flats, and it was much colder than it had been in town.

We pulled off at a turnout where we could view the river from the warmth of the truck. Rising fish were everywhere

(YNP) = Yellowstone National Park

and we knew we had no choice but to brave the elements. Knowing it might be our last chance to fish the Firehole for the year made it a little easier.

We decided to cross the river to keep the wind at our backs, which would allow us to fish a bit longer before hypothermia set in. Our presentations would also be helped if we could cast with the wind. Emerging *Baetis punctiventris* (Bee'-tiss punk-tuh-ven'-triss) mayflies covered the surface and they were exactly what we had expected to see. This *Baetis* species is the last important hatch of the year, and trout rose steadily to the tiny duns all around us.

By drifting size #22 Sparkle Duns over the trout we managed to fool several fish. Just enough fish, in fact, that our hands got thoroughly soaked. In short order the cold and wind completely numbed our wet hands. When one of us (we'll never tell who) finally executed a nice swan dive into the river, we knew the Fat Lady had sung. We piled into the truck, fired the heater up, and called it a season.

The genus *Baetis* has recently undergone major taxonomic revisions. In older fly fishing books, the mayfly *Pseudocloeon edmundsi* (Sue-doe-clee'-on ed-munds'-eye) is often noted as being important in this area. *Pseudocloeon* is no longer recognized as a genus, and the species *P. edmundsi* is now considered synonymous with *Baetis punctiventris*.

Baetis punctiventris thrives in three of our rivers: the Firehole and Madison in Yellowstone Park, and the Henry's Fork. On the Henry's Fork this fly is a significant food source for small trout, but the larger fish don't seem to feed on them. *Baetis punctiventris* is an exceptionally valuable food source on the Madison and Firehole rivers for trout of all sizes. In fact, for fishermen this is one of only three important mayfly hatches on these two rivers (the others are the Pale Morning Dun and *Baetis tricaudatus*).

Baetis punctiventris emerges heavily in May, June, September, and October on the Madison and Henry's Fork. On the Firehole *B. punctiventris* emerges year-round, but major peaks occur in the same spring and fall months as on the other rivers. Daily emergence takes place anytime from 10:00 a.m. until 5:00 p.m. in both good and bad weather, though like other mayflies the heaviest emergences occur in inclement conditions.

The nymphs of this mayfly are tiny, ranging from size #20 to #26. They are a bright, pale green in color and have the same streamlined shape as *Baetis tricaudatus*. They are excellent swimmers. The nymphs are unimportant in fishing, even though like *Baetis tricaudatus* they emerge at the surface. We are not sure why, but the Firehole and Madison River fish do not seem to concentrate on the emerging nymphs the way they sometimes will with *Baetis tricaudatus*.

Baetis punctiventris duns are two tailed, range in size from #20 to #26, and vary widely in color. Female duns typically have bright green bodies; the male's are usually shades of gray or brown. Both sexes have pale gray wings.

Spinners have clear wings and either bright green bodies (females) or brown bodies (males). Spinner falls take place in either morning or evening.

The overriding consideration in fishing this *Baetis*, whether with duns or spinners, is current speed. While these mayflies emerge and fall on all stretches of the Firehole and Madison, fish will only feed on them where it is beneficial to do so. That is, a trout will instinctively not expend more energy in capturing these tiny flies than it gains from eating them. Smooth, slow to moderate flows are prerequisites for finding fish feeding on these *Baetis*. Examples of ideal water are Muleshoe Bend on the Firehole and the mile or so of water below Seven Mile Bridge on the Madison. Where appropriate water is found both duns and spinners will be taken eagerly by trout.

Because these *Baetis* vary so much in size and color, an exact match in fly is not critical to success. We prefer to fish size #22 imitations, and most often tie them in bright green. A Sparkle Dun is a good choice of pattern during emergences, and a Sparkle Spinner will suffice for any spinner fall.

Selected emergences:
> Firehole: Year-round, with peaks in May, June, September and October
> Madison (YNP): June, September and October
> Henry's Fork: June, September and October

Rhithrogena

Rhithrogena (Rith-row-gene'-uh) is the first large mayfly of the year to emerge, but it is present in fishable numbers only on the Henry's Fork. (Though technically outside our area, there are good populations in the Madison around Beartrap Canyon, and the Gallatin west of Bozeman.) This early season species is *Rhithrogena morrisoni* (more-uh-so'-nigh), and begins emerging around the 20th of May on the Henry's Fork. It is a mid-morning mayfly, and both duns and spinners often appear on the water simultaneously around 10:30 or 11:00 a.m. The fish will feed on both the dun and spinner stages, and this activity typically lasts one to two hours.

Freshly emerged duns range in size from #14 to #16, and have a pale olive body, light gray wings with strong, dark venation, and two tails. There is some speculation that they emerge from their nymphal shucks under the surface, and our experience does not refute this. We have seen few cripples at the surface, and the successful duns appear full-blown on the water. No shedding of shucks or struggling with the unfolding of wings—perfect specimens just appear instantaneously, which lends some support to the theory of underwater emergence.

Rhithrogena morrisoni spinners are the same size as the duns, with the typically clear wings and brownish bodies of most spinners. They also have two tails, and can usually be seen swarming over the river banks early in the morning before mating.

The nymphs of *R. morrisoni* and related species all have three tails, are flattened in appearance, and the gills on body segments one and seven meet beneath the abdomen to form a disc. This latter feature is readily apparent when viewed from underneath. From a fishing standpoint, we have never found it necessary to be concerned with imitating the nymphs.

Two other species of *Rhithrogena, futilis* (few-till'-iss) and *undulata* (und-jew-lay'-tuh), can be seen in quantity on other rivers. The Gallatin, Madison, and Yellowstone all have excellent populations of these insects, but the only important stage on these rivers is spinners. We have not yet seen enough emerging duns at any one time to consider them an important phase. The spinner falls can be heavy, however, and stimulate good rises of trout. These can occur on calm, warm evenings from the middle of July until early September. Both *R. futilis* and *R. undulata* spinners are size #16, and their bodies range from an almost colorless, opaque look to light brown to almost black. We have not found color to be a critical factor in imitating the spinners.

The patterns we use to imitate *Rhithrogena* duns are a Sparkle Dun and a soft hackled emerger for the *R. morrisoni* emergence on the Henry's Fork. Even though the Sparkle Dun is an emerging dun pattern, and emerging duns are not seen on the river surface, the fish still accept them readily. A standard spinner tie in any of the colors we have mentioned, and the correct size, is sufficient when a spinner fall is encountered.

Selected emergences:
    Henry's Fork: May 25 - June 15
    Yellowstone: July 15 - September 5
    Gallatin: July - August
    Madison: July - August

Pale Morning Dun

The Pale Morning Dun is arguably the single most important insect to fly fishermen in the Yellowstone area. Pale

Morning Duns are certainly the most important mayfly; they inhabit every trout stream and are *the* major hatch on most. Each phase of their life cycle is fed upon heavily by trout, and they emerge continuously from May through August. No other insect can make that claim. A knowledge of Pale Morning Duns can do nothing but aid an angler fishing the summer months.

Fishing a good Pale Morning Dun emergence can be a profound experience. Our minds overflow with memories of early June days spent fishing the Firehole, while the river poured forth wave after wave of duns. Trout often fed for hours, smallish rainbows splashily rising in the middle of the stream as well as big browns barely wrinkling the surface along a protected bank. It was possible to fish leisurely, enjoying the sheer spectacle of Yellowstone blossoming into spring. Time was always on our side; the season was young and many more emergences were yet to come. Days ten years past are still fresh in the memory.

Then too, there are the spinner falls. What can compare to a late summer evening spent on the smooth flats of the Yellowstone? The tall, bankside conifers shadow the river early, and a heightened sense of anticipation prevails as the afternoon wind drops. Without warning, fish that had been rising intermittently suddenly develop regular, sustained rhythms. In mere minutes the entire river comes alive as more cutthroat join in. A glance at the surface reveals thousands of Pale Morning spinners, and we always wonder how they got there without our first noticing them in the air.

During the spinner fall the trout feed for hours, paying fishermen no mind at all, and while we often catch a few, it is never as many as we think we should. It is impossible to leave feeling that you've mastered the situation. Perhaps it should be this way, for that is exactly what keeps us coming back.

Two mayfly species make up the Pale Morning Dun experience; *Ephemerella infrequens* (Uh-fem-er-el'-la in-free'-kwens) and *Ephemerella inermis* (in-er'-mis). Both species look alike, except in size. Duns of both species exhibit wide variations in body color. Luckily, a strict determination of species is unnecessary since both flies have similar behavioral patterns.

Generally speaking, *E. infrequens* is the first of the two to emerge in the season, doing so from the end of May through June. They are larger than *E. inermis*; size #14 to #16 is the common range of the nymphs and adults. *Ephemerella inermis* is size #18 most often, but can be as small as #20. Their emergence takes place from mid-June through August.

Because the two species look and act alike they can be treated as one—simply, the Pale Morning Dun. The nymphs are three tailed crawlers, and range in color from amber to brown to almost black. Populations can reach incredible densities in good habitat; we have seined several hundred individuals from just a square foot of gravel bottom on the Henry's Fork.

The duns are stately looking mayflies, with three tails, well proportioned bodies and wings, and a body color spectrum that encompasses everything from pastel green to bright yellow to orange and on to a rich mahogany. Much of this variation in color is sexually dependent. Female duns are typically lighter and more subdued in color than the males. The wings of all Pale Morning Duns are pale gray.

Pale Morning Dun spinners have three tails and clear wings. The female spinners have olive bodies, the male's are a rusty brown in color.

Each phase of the life cycle of the Pale Morning Dun provides tremendous angling opportunities. The nymphs are readily available as they ascend to the surface and as they drift in the surface film prior to shedding their shucks. Large trout frequently feed only on the nymphs during emergence.

Then too, the successful transformation from nymph to dun is never a given either. Deformed and stillborn duns are common enough that trout often feed exclusively on them, knowing full well how vulnerable these flies are. Successfully emerged Pale Morning Duns sometimes ride the water for long distances, providing trout another chance to take them.

The spinner stage is extremely important for both anglers and trout too. Pale Morning spinners fall in the morning, evening, or, frequently, both morning and evening.

Besides presenting so many varying opportunities for fly fishermen and trout, Pale Morning Dun activity is remarkably predictable and consistent. When they are in season and the daily weather is conducive, you can count on their presence.

Because Pale Morning Duns emerge from May through August it is impossible to assign a time of day to expect them. In general they emerge at the most comfortable time of the day. On a snowy June day on the Firehole that means around noon or 1:00 p.m., when the temperature peaks for the day. A bright, hot day in July on the Henry's Fork may find Pale Mornings emerging as early as 9:00 a.m. in an effort to avoid the heat of the day. 11:00 a.m. is probably most typical on a day without unusual weather circumstances—by then the early morning chill is out of the air, and the heat of the day is still several hours away. Emergences can last from thirty minutes to over three hours.

Spinner falls can be expected on calm mornings and/or evenings. Normal time frames are between 9:00 a.m. and 11:00 a.m. and from 7:00 p.m. to 10:30 p.m. As with the emergences, there is a tendency for the spinners to choose the most comfortable time within the ranges we have given.

When fishing an emergence, it is necessary to carry nymph and dun patterns. We carry two kinds of nymph, depending on where we are fishing. One type is tied so it can be fished subsurface, the other is tied to float. On the Firehole and Henry's Fork, for example, the fish often prefer to take nymphs in the surface film, in which case we use the floating pattern. The big, wary fish in the Madison—mostly brown trout between sixteen and twenty inches—invariably ignore floating flies of any kind during this hatch. They still feed actively, but only on drifting nymphs. Situations like this call for a subsurface pattern that sinks roughly four to six inches. An unweighted Pheasant Tail nymph works well.

The dun pattern we prefer is the Sparkle Dun. This fly is a good representation of an emerging dun, or a dun trapped in its shuck. Fish sometimes key in on this stage and a good imitation can make all the difference. Even when fish may be taking fully emerged duns, we still use a Sparkle Dun. We are convinced that trout recognize crippled or otherwise impaired duns and, whether or not they are currently feeding on them, almost always accept an imitation of one.

It is difficult, but sometimes necessary, to determine whether trout are taking nymphs or duns. In certain holding spots fish may see more of one than the other drifting by, and may develop a selectivity to one stage. Watching naturals drift over a trout and seeing them taken is obviously the best indication of dun feeding. Noses and heads breaking the water are another likely sign of dun feeding. If the fish continues feeding as duns pass overhead, think nymphs. If backs and tails, or just tails alone are seen, nymphs are almost surely being taken.

Pale Morning Dun spinners are best imitated with a pale olive or rusty Sparkle Spinner. We don't believe we have witnessed a time when the trout preferred one color, but we still carry and use both. Trout can be extremely tough to catch when they lock onto spinners and we aren't ruling out the possibility that color may be involved.

Selected emergences:
Firehole: May 10 - July 8
Madison (YNP): May 5 - July 8
Henry's Fork: June 1 - July 30
Madison: June 25 - August 13
Slough Creek: July 1 - July 20
Yellowstone River: July 15 - September 5

Green Drake

The Green Drake is one of Yellowstone's best known mayflies, but most fishermen associate them with only the Henry's Fork River. While the Henry's Fork does have the most famous emergence, many other rivers in the area count Green Drakes among their major hatches. The Yellowstone, Lamar, Slough Creek, Soda Butte, and Gallatin rivers all come to mind when Green Drake talk begins.

Green Drakes can be found emerging from June through September on these various rivers. The explanation for this lengthy emergence schedule is that historically several mayfly species have been grouped under the Green Drake name. These mayflies are all closely related taxonomically, but vary in appearance and the time of year they emerge. The important species on the Henry's Fork and Yellowstone is *Drunella grandis* (Drew-nell'-uh gran'-diss). *Drunella doddsi* (dodds'-eye), *Drunella coloradensis* (col-lar-uh-den'-sis), and *Timpanoga hecuba* (Tim-pan-o'-guh heck-you'-buh) are significant on the Lamar, Soda Butte, and Slough Creek. All four species are present in the Gallatin.

The Henry's Fork has perhaps the best population of Green Drakes, and its emergence occurs soonest in the year. Late June is the time.

The Yellowstone hatch is the shortest lived and most difficult to meet. Green Drakes will emerge on just two to four of the last ten days in July. It is impossible to predict on which of these days the Drakes will emerge, but should a cloudy, rainy day arise during this period, drop everything and head for the river. This will be your best chance to see and fish an emergence.

Slough Creek, Soda Butte, and the Lamar River all experience their Green Drake emergences in the fall. September is the prime month, and because little other insect activity will then be taking place on these rivers, the trout take advantage of every emergence. The Green Drake species here don't seem as abundant as those on the other rivers, and sparse emergences are more frequent than heavy ones. Keep in mind, however, that it does not take many duns to bring up the trout.

One other important point: the distribution of Green Drakes on Slough, Soda Butte, and the Lamar is fragmented. Certain stretches will have good numbers, others will be completely barren, and it may be necessary to move around until the bugs are found. Too, these changes can be yearly, a probable consequence of the stream-altering, torrential runoff these streams experience.

The dun stage of the Green Drake is of primary concern to

anglers, and there are several shared characteristics among these species. All have a stocky, heavy build. They are large in size; #10 to #12 is the typical range. Three tails and large dark gray wings are also universal features. Body color is the obvious difference among the duns, and this varies widely, even within the same species. Green, yellow, olive, brown, and reddish-brown are all exhibited to various degrees.

Green Drake nymphs are large (#8 to #10 at maturity), with stocky bodies, three tails, and stout legs. They range in color from olive to all shades of brown. They are crawling flies, and clumsy ones at that. Fish may be caught on their imitations, but we don't consider one necessary.

Likewise, we consider Green Drake spinners to be unimportant. As a rule, their falls occur in the early morning hours when it is still dark. We don't know anyone who has actually ventured forth to find and fish a spinner fall. We have witnessed just three or four spinner falls in the last fifteen years, and these occurred around 7:30 a.m. following unusual early morning fogs. Green Drake spinners have clear, glassy wings, but otherwise resemble the duns.

Green Drake emergences generally occur between 10:00 a.m. and 1:00 p.m.; truly civilized hours! Trout may be suspicious of these large flies at the beginning of each year's emergence, but once they do start feeding on them it takes only a few individuals to elicit interest from the fish. Even the sparsest of hatches will bring some nice fish up to the surface. And, though it may take a day or two at the beginning of the hatch for the trout to recognize these huge flies as food, fish can be caught on Green Drake imitations for over a week after their emergence has ended.

In extremely heavy hatches, trout will often bypass the fully emerged duns in favor of floating nymphs and emerging duns. During sparse hatches it is likely they will eat all the Drakes that float by, fully emerged or otherwise. For all our Green Drake fishing, the pattern we use is the Green Drake Emerger. It has worked unfailingly in all the Drake situations we have encountered, regardless of whether the trout were eating emergers or duns.

Selected emergences:

Henry's Fork: June 15 - July 6
Yellowstone: July 20 - July 31
Lamar and Soda Butte: August 25 - September 15
Slough Creek: August 30 - September 30

Brown Drake

The end of June is our favorite time to fish the Gibbon River. This is Brown Drake time, and the emergences of these huge mayflies bring up the largest fish in the river. These fish are typically brown trout, and only when the Brown Drakes are out can you expect to see them surface feeding. The rest of their time is spent foraging in the deep holes and hiding beneath the banks. One of our most memorable experiences with this hatch occurred a couple of seasons ago.

We had arrived at the upper meadow at 6:00 p.m., amidst an impressive thunder and lightning display. As we started to put our waders on, rain began falling steadily, and we wondered if we would even get a chance to fish. After watching the river for awhile from the truck and seeing no rises, we finally decided to walk out for a closer inspection. Warm rain still poured from the sky, but we figured that was why we had rain jackets, so off we went.

We took our time and sloshed the half mile up to Lily Pad pool. The rain eased a bit on our arrival at the pool, but there was still no fish or insect activity. Around 7:00 p.m. the rain stopped, and an eerie stillness overtook the meadow. Thick, black clouds hung ominously and a premature darkness set in. Five minutes later, all hell broke loose.

Brown Drakes were popping up everywhere, and the trout wasted no time in getting on them. The normally reserved big browns threw caution to the wind, gobbling every bug that came their way. They rose right at our feet as we stood on the bank. We calmly decided to just stand and watch, foregoing any fishing in order to enjoy the spectacle...ha!

We actually turned into two madmen as the first trout began feeding. In desperate haste, we made bad cast after bad cast. We slapped the water, dragged our flies, hit the fish on the head, but it didn't matter. The trout could not be put down. We never looked back and we had ourselves a field day.

Brown Drakes, *Ephemera simulans*, (Uh-fem'-er-uh sim-you'- lans), inhabit two rivers in this area in fishable numbers: the Gibbon and Henry's Fork. Their habitat requirements affect their distribution; the nymphs are burrowing mayflies, living in U-shaped tunnels they hollow out in the river bottom. Consequently, they need a fairly fine substrate into which they can dig. The upper meadows on the Gibbon, and the slower stretches in the Railroad Ranch section of the Henry's Fork are two examples of prime Brown Drake habitat.

Brown Drakes are large mayflies; nymphs and adults run from size #8 to #12. The nymphs are three tailed, slender, and have prominent feathery gills. Their color is typically a light brownish-yellow.

Brown Drake duns and spinners are striking in appearance. Besides being large, they have heavily mottled wings; dun wings are gray flecked with dark brown, spinner wings are clear with dark brown mottling. The bodies of both are light brown with dark brown rings at the end of each body segment. Both duns and spinners have three tails.

Emergences of Brown Drakes generally take place in the evenings during late June and July. Though we have seen emergences as early as 4:00 p.m., 7:00 p.m. to 10:00 p.m. is a more typical time frame. At this time of year total darkness doesn't set in until after 10:00 p.m., and it is sometimes necessary to stay onstream this late to catch the best action.

Brown Drake nymphs are adequate swimmers. The rise forms often made by fish feeding during a Brown Drake emergence, particularly on the Henry's Fork, leave little doubt that the trout are taking nymphs. The rises are subsurface in origin, sometimes quiet, sometimes aggressive, and usually leave an impressive swirl on the surface. Our success with a nymph pattern is usually equally unimpressive. Even when we catch fish, it feels like it is more by accident than by design.

In various fly fishing books, much has been made about the undulating body motion with which the nymphs swim. Many fly patterns have been suggested to imitate this movement, as if this feature is the trigger the trout respond to. These patterns and all others we have tried have been largely ineffective for us. We feel there are other triggers that the trout look for, even though we're not certain what they are.

The trout on the Henry's Fork move around a lot while feeding, which complicates presentation (did that trout see any of my last dozen casts?). But even taking this into account we can't avoid a feeling of underachievement during many emergences when the fish are feeding on nymphs. There are obviously other factors at work, and this is one hatch that can still use more study.

At times we have had great success with emergers and duns, even when the fish are nymphing, but we cannot explain why. This is one of the ongoing mysteries of the Brown Drake hatch. Carry nymphs, emergers and duns and try them all; that's our best advice for fishing an emergence of this mayfly.

Spinner falls of Brown Drakes occur in the evening, though they are highly unpredictable, especially on the Gibbon. This is another mystery peculiar to Brown Drakes. We have witnessed tremendous emergences of Drakes one evening and have then returned to the stream for four or five consecutive evenings hoping to catch the spinner fall, all to no avail.

It isn't that we don't find the spinners, for they can be observed swarming by the thousands. The spinners are first seen hovering at tree top height in early evening and as the night progresses they descend lower and lower. Eventually, the spinners are dancing just above the surface and it appears as if all is set for a glorious spinner fall. Then, in a brief moment, the spinners completely vanish.

We know from sampling these swarms that they are comprised mostly of males, which is nothing extraordinary in mayfly behavior. What is unusual is that the females never seem to show themselves. We have witnessed this time and again, all under ostensibly ideal conditions.

Swarming behavior is a prelude to mating in most mayfly species. Females typically enter the swarm of males, mate, and then lay their eggs. No mating appears to be taking place in our observed Brown Drake swarms. It is possible that mating activity and egglaying occur well after dark when no fishermen are around, but we have seen enough falls during the early evening hours that we don't feel these occurrences were something out of the ordinary. The unpredictability of Brown Drake spinner falls is simply still a mystery to us.

When we *have* encountered good spinner falls the trout have eaten them readily, and fly pattern seems to be less important than presentation. You must cast your fly so that it floats dragfree over the trout in synch with his natural feeding rhythm.

Selected emergences:
 Henry's Fork: June 20 - July
 Gibbon River: June 21 - July 10

Flavs

Along with Brown Drakes, Flavs are the only other mayfly of importance here that emerge in the evening. But unlike Brown Drakes, Flavs are far more widespread and numerous; they are one of this area's most significant summer mayfly hatches. Flavs are a sizable mayfly, capable of bringing up the largest fish in a river to surface feed. Their emergences hold few secrets too; Flav hatches are often responsible for some of this area's easiest dry fly fishing. The name Flav is derived from their Latin name, *Drunella flavilinea* (Drew-nell'-uh flav-uh-lin-ee'-uh).

Flavs are found in abundance on the following rivers: Henry's Fork, Yellowstone, the Firehole, and the Madison below Quake Lake. Depending on the river, emergences can occur anytime from the middle of June to the middle of August. The time of day to expect a hatch varies considerably depending on the weather. On sunny, warm summer days Flavs will begin emerging around sunset or a short while on either side. At this latitude in July that means sometime between 8:00 p.m. and 10:00 p.m. When weather conditions are rainy, cool, or heavily overcast, Flavs often appear much earlier; 5:00 p.m. or 6:00 p.m. is typical, and we have seen them emerge in good numbers as early as 3:00 p.m. Emergences last anywhere from thirty minutes to two hours.

Inclement weather always seems to prompt the heaviest emergences and the best rises of fish. We look forward to rain, wind, and cold because they almost insure good Flav activity. Ironically, these same conditions drive most anglers from the stream just when they should be starting.

Last July, for instance, we hit a brief but superb emergence on the Madison. We had arrived at the Cliff and Wade Lake bridge at five o'clock in the afternoon in a light drizzle and cool breeze. We proceeded to string our rods as several groups of fishermen around us shed their gear and headed home. Most of the anglers leaving had spent the whole day on the river, and when it started raining around dinner time, they decided to call it quits. Those we visited with thought we must be crazy to fish under these conditions, but past experiences encouraged us to stick around. After all, it was still early.

By six o'clock the rain ceased, and another one of those infamous eerie calms surrounded us. It felt as though we were in the eye of a hurricane. The mountains were still blanketed with storm clouds, and in the early darkness we had a sense that something big was about to happen. The air felt warmer in the calm, and a brief moment later the river pockets were filled with drifting Flavs. Fish began working immediately and so did we.

We fished intensely, for we had been in many of these situations before and knew that rain and wind could start again anytime, putting a damper on the hatch and the feeding activity. We cast to the biggest fish we saw, and our Sparkle Duns were taken without hesitation. Our catch included more brown trout than rainbows, a rarity for the Madison, but one that reveals the power of this emergence, plus early darkness, to lure out even the normally shy, nocturnal browns.

Flavs are sometimes referred to as Small Western Green Drakes, a descriptive but ungainly name. With olive bodies, dark gray wings and three tails the duns superficially resemble their Green Drake cousins. Flavs, however, run from size #14 to #16. Spinners have clear wings, a dark olive to olive brown body, and three tails.

Flav nymphs are stocky, three tailed crawlers, and they can be found in all shades of brown.

Flavs emerge at the surface and fish generally feed on the drifting duns. Finding fish concentrating on the nymphs is rare, and we almost never use a nymph imitation. Our favorite pattern is the Sparkle Dun, an emerging dun imitation. Even though Flavs are not as prone to emergence defects as, say, Pale Morning Duns, emerger patterns still work well.

Flav spinners fall in the evenings and, when concentrated alone, can stimulate good rises of fish. Flav spinners are often overshadowed by the simultaneous emergence of caddisflies, particularly on the Madison and Yellowstone. Still, it is wise to carry appropriate imitations. Flav emergences and spinner falls are unlikely to coincide, for when an emergence takes place on a nice, warm evening it will probably occur after any spinner fall has occurred. And, while inclement weather can stimulate excellent emergences, it will preclude any spinners from falling.

Selected emergences:
Firehole: June 10 - June 25
Henry's Fork: June 24 - July 25
Madison: July 15 - August 10
Yellowstone: July 20 - August 10

Gray Drake

Slough Creek lies in the most scenic part of Yellowstone, meandering first through small, alpine meadows, then plunging through a tight gorge and eventually spilling into the wide open, sagebrush covered Lamar valley. The Beartooth Mountains cut a jagged horizon in the distance, and the land is prime elk, buffalo, and grizzly bear habitat. An angler's first look at the river, however, is likely to be as uninspiring as his first glances at the surrounding scenery prove inspiring. It looks like anything but the incredibly productive trout water it is.

The lower meadow section of the river is full of long, deep, silty, slow pools, interspersed with short riffles. The upper meadows are mostly unbroken stretches of slow-flowing, meandering water, with huge depositions of glacial sand on the inside of every corner. Scoured out, crumbling banks are a common sight; an unfortunate testament to the torrential runoff the whole river suffers in June.

But the appearance of the river belies it's productivity, for it contains a wealth of fish and insect life. The trout are cutthroat and rainbows, sculpin abound in the riffles, and all variety of important mayflies are plentiful. One of these, the Gray Drake, is especially significant.

The Gray Drake, *Siphlonurus occidentalis* (Siff-lo-nur'-us ox-uh-den-tay'-lis), is Slough's largest mayfly, about a size #10, and they emerge from early July through the middle of September. Excellent populations are also present on the Yellowstone River, Yellowstone Lake, and the Henry's Fork below Ashton. *Siphlonurus* emerges from July through the middle of September.

Siphlonurus nymphs are superb swimmers. Their three feathery tails, strong abdomens, and streamlined shapes allow them to move quickly through the water in short bursts. Mature nymphs congregate and emerge along shore, never really exposing themselves to the trout, which obviously limits their significance in fishing. Many nymphs actually crawl out of the water onto weeds or logs to complete emergence.

Siphlonurus occidentalis duns are two tailed, with light gray wings and pale olive to tan bodies. There are dark brown rings at the rear of each body segment. As with the nymphs, the duns are relatively insignificant. Unless a strong wind is blowing, forcing the duns away from the shore where they emerged, fish can't take advantage of them. They also have a tendency to emerge sporadically throughout the day, never giving the trout a chance to get tuned into them.

The spinner stage is a different story. The morning falls are well coordinated, with hordes of Drakes swarming over and then falling to the water surface. These concentrated falls give the trout every opportunity to feed, and feed heavily they do. *Siphlonurus* bring up the largest fish to surface feed, and this activity takes place from approximately 10:00 a.m. to 12:00 noon. If conditions are right, there will be occasional falls in the evening too; this is something we see frequently on the Yellowstone.

The *S. occidentalis* spinner has two tails and a tannish body with distinctive dark brown horseshoe markings on the underside of their abdomen. Like all spinners the wings are clear.

Because of the size of these mayflies, fish can be a little shy about taking the spinners, and we always use fine tippets and sparsely tied patterns. The take itself is invariably slow and deliberate, so a careful strike is essential. It is very easy to strike too quickly, especially on the Yellowstone and Slough Creek, where the cutthroat trout are naturally slow takers to begin with.

Selected emergences:
   Slough Creek: July 1 - September 17
   Yellowstone River: July 18 - September 15
   Yellowstone Lake: July
   Henry's Fork: late June - July

Callibaetis

The morning was half over by the time Ronnie Hall met us at Gus's Diner. Ronnie likes to keep gentlemen's hours during fishing season, and if our plan hadn't been to go gulper fishing on Hebgen Lake, we would have left without him long before. But gulper fishing can be gentlemanly too, especially when matching the late morning *Callibaetis* (Cal-uh-bee'-tiss) mayfly activity, so we ate a leisurely breakfast confident we weren't missing a thing.

Our watches showed eleven o'clock when we pulled in at Frank's Point on Hebgen's Madison Arm. The lake was still smooth as glass, and *Callibaetis* spinners were swarming over the bank. While most float tubers were out in the middle of the arm chasing the remnants of the early morning midge emergence, we knew the impending *Callibaetis* activity would be confined to the weedbeds just offshore, and that this would be the place to be.

Fish were beginning to feed steadily as we eased our float tubes into the lake. The audible gulping sound that rainbows and browns make when feeding on the surface (hence their nickname "gulpers"), could be heard for a hundred yards. There were great numbers of *Callibaetis* spinners falling to the surface, and the trout were coming in close to shore to feed on them.

As we paddled out among the weed beds, Ronnie immediately hooked a trout not fifteen feet from shore while trying to get into his tube. He promptly landed a nice rainbow, and had barely seated himself in his tube when he hooked another. It turned out to be a good morning for the three of us as we fished in and around the emergent weedbeds. This is perfect *Callibaetis* habitat, and with plenty of emerging duns and spinners available, trout concentrate their feeding efforts on these spots.

A knowledge of insects and their behavior was invaluable in this instance. It allowed us to fish where the fish were feeding, instead of paddling around the middle of the Madison Arm with nothing to cast to, which was the fate that befell many anglers that morning.

Callibaetis mayflies are largely stillwater insects. In this area, there are tremendous numbers in such lakes as Hebgen, Wade, Hidden, and Yellowstone. Local ponds and sloughs also contain excellent populations. The only river with a fishable population is the Henry's Fork, and there the *Callibaetis* are primarily concentrated in the slower stretches of the Railroad Ranch.

There is one species of *Callibaetis* in this area, and that is *Callibaetis americanus* (uh-mare-uh-con'-us). *Callibaetis coloradensis* (col-lar-uh-den'-sis) and *Callibaetis nigritus* (nuh-gri'-tus), which most flyfishing books list as the important species, are now considered synonymous with *C. americanus* and are no longer recognized individually. The nymph, dun, and spinner stages of *C. americanus* are all significant trout foods.

Callibaetis nymphs generally inhabit weedbeds, and are superb swimmers. Their streamlined bodies and three feathery tails help them to dart about in characteristic six to eight inch spurts. Their size at maturity is #14 - #16, and body color is typically a mottled tannish-gray.

The duns are two-tailed, with bodies ranging from pale olive to cream to tan. This variation in color is in part a function of the particular environment they are found in. The wings are a highly distinctive mottled gray and brown. Size is #14 to #16.

The spinner stage of *Callibaetis* closely resembles the dun in size and color. The only exception is the wings, which are clear with brown mottling.

Callibaetis mayflies emerge in the late morning and early afternoon; 10:00 a.m. to 2:00 p.m. is the typical time frame. Spinner falls may occur anytime from 11:00 a.m. to 3:00 p.m. Because most of our *Callibaetis* fishing is done on lakes, there are some peculiarities involved that must be considered in order to be successful.

30

To begin with, trout often react to insects on a lake surface independently of the insects themselves. That is, the mere presence of insects on the surface, regardless of how susceptible they may be, does not mean the trout will be feeding on them. The presence and degree of wind (and there is never a shortage of wind in the west!) is a key factor in determining whether the trout will surface feed or not. Trout tend to surface feed avidly in lakes when the surface is smooth, and they can be reluctant to do so when wind ruffles the surface.

Under calm conditions, which are always the most desirable, several scenarios can occur. At the beginning of a *Callibaetis* emergence, you commonly see aggressive, splashy rises as the trout chase the swimming nymphs. There is rarely a pattern to the rise forms so it is difficult to tell where a fish is at any given moment. Blind nymphing is a viable tactic and should be done by casting around weedbeds and retrieving in short strips.

As the emergence intensifies and *Callibaetis* duns appear in number on the surface, many fish will be seen and heard linking rise forms together every couple of feet as they feed on the duns. This is the classic gulper situation. Our strategy is to single out one fish, note his direction of travel, and position ourselves so he passes within casting range. When paddling in a float tube to intercept a fish, it is critical to avoid creating too many waves. Gulpers are highly sensitive to these waves and will immediately change direction when they feel them. This always seems to happen just outside your maximum casting range.

Keeping false casting to a minimum, we lead the fish by the same distance he is traveling between gulps. This distance is usually a function of the number of *Callibaetis* on the water; the greater the number of naturals the shorter the distance between gulps. If all goes well, we strike gently to protect our 5x or 6x tippet. If the fish passes by our fly we pick up the line quietly, and with no false casts immediately present it again. Presentation is paramount; the fish are feeding rhythmically and are not apt to break their pattern or move side to side to take a fly.

Callibaetis spinner falls often coincide with the emergences. Trout will feed on the spinners as readily as the duns and generally show no preference for one or the other. Putting the fly in front of the fish is more important than fly pattern, and we generally fish a size #16 Adams, or size #16 *Callibaetis* Sparkle Dun.

As we said earlier, wind can play a significant role in fishing a *Callibaetis* emergence. Our typical summer winds are convection winds, the turbulent results of air masses changing temperature and altitude. They usually pick up sometime between 11:00 a.m. and 2:00 p.m., precisely the time to expect the heaviest *Callibaetis* activity. A rule of thumb we follow in fishing is that if the wind is blowing prior to any *Callibaetis* activity, then regardless of how many duns or spinners subsequently appear on the surface the trout will not feed on them. If the trout are already feeding on *Callibaetis* before the wind comes up, they will continue to feed in the wind as long as it does not become gale force.

A slight breeze can actually be extremely helpful because the lake surface becomes disturbed. Float tube waves will be cushioned quickly and your approach will be masked. The trout will not hold their paths as well either; side to side moves are common, and these create a larger target area to cast to. Gulping fish also seem less wary; they are not as easily put down by a bad cast.

Callibaetis mayflies can occasionally be seen emerging on area lakes as early as May, but the best emergences occur from July into September. This long emergence span is likely a consequence of *Callibaetis* mayflies being multibrooded. Late summer populations are the offspring of early summer broods.

Selected emergences:
    Hebgen Lake: May, July 15 - September 15
    Hidden Lake: mid-June - July
    Henry's Fork: August - September 15

Tricorythodes

A river full of rising fish on a bright, late August morning is a rare sight in the Yellowstone area. There are at least two reasons for this. One, most of the major insect hatches fish feed on have completed their yearly emergences. Two, warm August temperatures are not conducive to good emergences, and insect activity is generally confined to the cooler hours of early morning and late evening. But while it is unusual to find good morning activity, it is not impossible. A case in point is the Madison River in Yellowstone Park. There are tremendous rises of fish on most August mornings from the Barn's Pools downstream to Baker's Hole, and the insect responsible for this feeding is the *Tricorythodes* (Try-core-uh-tho'-dees) mayfly.

Over the years we have witnessed some gargantuan rises of fish on this stretch of the Madison; the water often resembles a hatchery pond at feeding time. The feeding fish are primarily whitefish, which may come as some disappointment to many anglers, but the sheer spectacle of so many rising fish should be seen by all anglers at least once. Too, the pods of whitefish shelter some fine trout which can make a morning's fishing interesting.

Tricorythodes mayflies are commonly referred to as "Tricos" by anglers, and there is only one species, *minutus* (my-new'-tus) in the genus that inhabits this area. Excellent Trico populations are found in the Madison in Yellowstone Park, the Madison Arm of Hebgen Lake, and the Henry's Fork River.

The species name *minutus* is an apt description of these bugs; they run from size #18 to #24. This considerable variation is a function of sex and distribution. On the Madison and Hebgen Lake, the females are as large as #18. Henry's Fork Tricos can be that large too but more often fall in the #20 to #22 range. Males on all three of these waters are smaller than the females, ranging from #20 to #24. Thankfully, the fish are never too fussy over this variation in size.

Trico nymphs have three tails and are typically dark brown in color. They inhabit silt bottoms and are not readily available to fish except at emergence. The duns and spinners also have three tails and no hind wings. Female duns are olive bodied; male duns have black bodies. Both sexes have light gray wings. Male and female spinners maintain their body color, but have clear wings, and exceptionally long tails.

Tricos have an unusual emergence and mating pattern. The males emerge in the evening and spend that night in the dun stage. The females emerge in the early morning and molt into spinners shortly thereafter. While the females are emerging, the males that emerged the previous night will molt and form huge mating swarms over the waters edge. As the females molt they fly back into the swarms of males and mate. Egglaying occurs promptly thereafter.

The primary fishing opportunities take place during the morning emergence of female duns and the subsequent spinner fall of both sexes. On Hebgen Lake, Tricos can be expected to emerge from 6:00 a.m. to 9:00 a.m. on the Madison Arm. Trout will feed primarily on the duns, and then only if the lake surface is glassy smooth; any wave action apparently inhibits their vision and they will not rise. As with *Callibaetis*, if enough duns are present the trout will establish a gulping rhythm, feeding in short, regular intervals and making an audible "gulp". This fishing is best done by float tube, and the same guidelines apply that we discussed in the *Callibaetis* section. Unlike *Callibaetis*, which favor the shoreline areas, the greatest number of Tricos can be found in the middle of the Madison Arm, away from shore.

The Trico spinner fall on Hebgen is not too significant. Spinners fall from mid-morning until noon, at the same time *Callibaetis* is emerging and egglaying, and the trout invariably prefer the larger mayflies. For those interested in fishing the Madison in the Park, the opposite is true. The spinner fall is the important stage here, and the emergence takes a back seat. As on Hebgen, the spinners fall around mid-morning.

On the Henry's Fork, Tricos are limited in distribution to

the slower, silty bottomed stretches, such as the Bonefish Flats area of the Railroad Ranch. Both emergences and spinner falls can be important. During emergence, which occurs in the early morning, rainbows will feed on emerging nymphs or duns. Individual fish will be found doing their own thing; some may take just nymphs, others just duns, and some fish may take both. Careful observation is required to discern whether duns are being selected. Visual tracking of individual duns is the best way to determine whether they're being eaten. If you can't see duns disappearing, it's a safe guess the trout are taking nymphs.

By mid-morning the spinners reach the water and all stages of Trico are often available at once to the fish. With millions of Tricos on the water it can be a tossup as to what fly to use. The tremendous numbers of bugs often get the rainbows hanging right in the film, gulping in a rapid rhythm, and in this situation presentation generally becomes more important than fly choice. Though the trout may be seeing mostly spinners at this point, we try to stick with a dun pattern and make them take it. A dun is easier to see on the water and lets us keep track of our casts and drifts.

Selected emergences:
    Hebgen Lake: June 25 - August 30
    Madison River: July 13 - September 15
    Henry's Fork: July 20 - September 15

Pink Lady

One late August afternoon we headed for Nez Perce Ford on the Yellowstone River. The daily buildup of thunderheads towered over the Park's interior, and the air had a sultry feel as we drove south from Canyon Junction. Luck was with us that day; there was no trace of wind and there were few other fishermen when we pulled in along the river. Most anglers had left for the afternoon, and who could blame them? Even on the Yellowstone, rising fish can be few and far between on a hot August afternoon.

We held out hope of greater things though, for a warm, overcast afternoon is perfect for an emergence of the Pink Lady. This mayfly normally emerges from around 5:00 p.m. to 7:00 p.m., but we knew that under cloudy conditions the emergence often gets pushed forward by a couple hours. True to our experience, we started seeing a few duns go floating by and fish starting to feed by 4:00 p.m. The afternoon fishermen had given up and vacated, and it was still a couple of hours before the evening anglers would arrive. The ability to take advantage of these small windows of opportunity is what a knowledge of insects provides, and we fared well that day.

The Pink Lady is a fast-water species of mayfly in the genus *Epeorus* (Ee-pee'-or-us). *Epeorus* nymphs have two tails, and are extremely flat in configuration; this body shape provides minimal water resistance and allows them to maintain a tenacious grip on rocks in even the swiftest of currents. The color of the nymphs varies from a pale watery olive to dark brown.

Epeorus albertae (al-ber'-tee) is the most important species in the genus. The name Pink Lady is derived from the body color of the female dun and spinner of this species. There is a strong pink cast to the bodies of *E. albertae*, one that can have tinges of orange as well. The male duns and spinners have pale olive bodies and both sexes have jet black eyes. Both duns and spinners have two tails. Wing color is pale gray for duns, and clear for spinners. The size of *E. albertae* nymphs and adults ranges from #12 to #14.

Epeorus mayflies are particularly interesting because of their unique emergence method. They shed their nymphal shuck near the bottom of the river and ascend to the surface as fully formed adults. As a result of this feature, the only flies that gain the surface are perfectly emerged duns, and these are the flies that the cutthroat key on. We have never seen cripples or partially emerged duns attain the surface.

Despite the fact that rising fish only feed on the perfect duns, we have had great success on the Yellowstone with soft hackle emergers and Sparkle Duns fished on the surface. This leads us to believe the fish do recognize emerging *Epeorus* and probably feed on them to some extent. We're guessing that during a given emergence trout either feed exclusively underneath or exclusively on the surface; we have never seen them make a switch from one to the other. We theorize that the trout simply recognize and accept an emerger, regardless of the level it is fished at.

An area largely unexplored is the use of wet fly patterns for western *Epeorus*. Though not essential for the Yellowstone, the strong possibility exists that on turbulent rivers like the Madison and Gallatin, wet fly patterns could outperform dry imitations. We know of no one who has spent enough time experimenting with them to indicate one way or another.

Rivers that have good populations besides the Yellowstone include the Gallatin, Madison, and Gardner. On all these waters, emergences of *Epeorus* are sparse compared to other mayflies. Don't expect to see the water covered with adults and likewise don't be put off by small numbers either; the sheer size alone of *Epeorus* is enough to get the trout feeding actively.

Selected emergences:
    Yellowstone: August 1 - September 4
    Other waters (sporadic): July - August

Attenella margarita

Every September, we hear stories from a parade of anglers about great mayfly hatches, lots of rising trout, and little fishing success. When we ask where they have been, the reply is usually "the Yellowstone around Buffalo Ford". Invariably, upon further questioning they describe the mayfly *Attenella margarita* (At-ten-el'-la mar-gar cyc' ta) to us, and memories of our own first encounter with this hatch come to mind.

On a cool September morning we had decided to fish the Yellowstone around Sulphur Cauldron, and as we walked down the hill to the river prior to stringing up, we could see there were already fish working. For us there's nothing worse than arriving onstream and seeing that there are already trout feeding. We are always overcome by a general state of frenzy—hurrying to get strung up (probably missing a guide in the process), tying bad knots and putting our waders on backwards.

At any rate, once we got successfully rigged we checked the river to see what was happening. The surface was covered with little olive mayflies, so we tied on appropriate dun patterns. After several minutes of futile casting (in most of these stories at least one small fish is caught, but we can't even lay claim to that) we finally settled down and paid attention to what was really occurring.

It turned out that what we thought were rises to adult mayflies were in reality trout eating nymphs at the surface. We discovered this by watching some visible fish in by shore; not only did they take nymphs at the surface, thereby creating what we thought was a surface rise, but they also fed regularly beneath the surface. These fish, often two to three feet down, left no indication on the surface that they even existed, let alone that they were actively feeding. They often fed eight or ten times underneath for every once at the surface. If we hadn't been able to watch them it would have appeared that considerably fewer fish were feeding than there really were and that they fed less frequently than they actually did.

We saw plenty of nymphal shucks drifting by us, and since an #18 Pheasant Tail nymph was a close match, we each tied one on. We then proceeded (as is usually the case in these stories) to catch a few fish, but only those we could see. This nymphing behavior is what causes most anglers fits when they fish this emergence, and indeed, it can be challenging fishing.

That incident was many years ago, but it and others since

then have taught us much about catching cutthroat feeding on *A. margarita* nymphs. The obvious lesson, and one worth remembering for many hatches, is this: because there are adults on the surface, it does not follow that rising fish are feeding on them.

More importantly, we learned that because the fish feed largely beneath the surface on *A. margarita*, and move so much during feeding, it is imperative to fish to visible trout. A cutthroat may feed in one spot, drift back fifteen feet, feed again, move to the side ten feet, feed, and so on. This behavior obviously limits the success of blind casting or casting to a rise form. They simply don't stay put when eating *A. margarita* nymphs or duns.

Attenella margarita are found most abundantly in smooth water, and since it is important to see the fish you are trying for, slick water is a great benefit. The flat water above LeHardy Rapids, around Buffalo Ford, and in the Sulphur Cauldron area are ideal spots.

Paying attention to the light, however, is even more critical to really mastering this emergence. There is usually some angle of approach to the fish where the sunlight helps you to see into the water, and that is where we fish from. Often it means wading out in the river and fishing back to the bank, sometimes it means fishing upstream, sometimes down. Our whole strategy is based on this; we do whatever it takes and go wherever we have to in order to see the cutthroat and keep track of their movement.

Our nymph patterns are unweighted to allow them to be fished at any depth. A fish that is feeding two feet under the surface one second may be in the surface film the next, and the only way to handle this is with an unweighted fly. If depth is required we accomplish it by casting further upstream of the trout, giving the fly more time to sink. Many times the fish will move before your fly reaches him, but this is all part of the game. Anticipating the fish's direction is sometimes possible by close observation. When the fish is at the surface you cast close, and the unweighted fly never runs the risk of drifting beneath him. Regardless of the depth, all our presentations are made drag-free on 6x tippet.

Since the drift is natural, a trout's take will not be felt. Sight must be relied upon, and we watch the trout closely for any feeding indications. We judge from the current speed where our fly is likely to be, and if we see our trout open his mouth, tip up, tip down, or move to the side we strike gently. Many times you guess wrong, but you still must strike on any indication. This is difficult fishing, and as experience is gained success eventually rises.

As can be seen from their picture, *A. margarita* nymphs have a typical Ephemerellid look. Their color varies from light amber to dark brown, and their size is #18.

The duns have medium gray wings, and bright olive to olive brown bodies. Like the nymphs, they have three tails. They are subject to many emergence defects, and on those rare occasions when the cutthroat feed on deformed duns we use a Sparkle Dun pattern.

Female spinners, which have olive bodies, are sometimes seen on the water, usually in the company of other species. The male spinners have translucent abdomens and black thoraxes. It would be rare to see either sex in large numbers, and we tie no specific patterns for either. A size #18 olive spinner will suffice if a spinner fall is encountered.

Selected emergence:
Yellowstone River: August 18 - October 4

Serratella tibialis

Like its cousin *Attenella margarita*, this mayfly is significant only on the Yellowstone. *Serratella tibialis* (Sair-uh-tell'-uh tib-ee-al'-iss) is an autumn mayfly too, and in fact often emerges concurrently with *Attenella margarita* on September days. On the water the two duns appear similar, but *S. tibialis* is actually slightly larger and darker than *A. margarita*. These may seem like minor points, but the fish will sometimes show a preference for one species when both are present.

Serratella tibialis duns are a small #16 in size, with dark gray wings, brown to brownish-olive bodies, cream legs, and three tails. Like other Ephemerellids, they often have trouble emerging from their shucks, and deformed duns are common. The Yellowstone cutthroat will eat the duns, but generally prefer the ascending nymphs. As with *A. margarita*, we feel that ease of capture and a general suspicion of floating flies this time of year are responsible for this strong preference towards nymphs. *Serratella tibialis* nymphs are similar to those of *A. margarita*; the two cannot be separated without a microscope. The nymphs of *S. tibialis* range from a pale mottled yellow to dark brown in color, and are size #16. Since the naturals vary so widely in color, the color of your imitation is not critical and we typically fish medium brown imitations.

What *is* highly critical is how the fly is fished. In fishing this emergence, if the trout are taking duns, standard dry fly tactics and 6x tippets are in order. If, as is usually the case, they are feeding on the nymphs, we use the same tactics as discussed for *Attenella margarita*. That is, try to work to visible fish, present your nymph at the level they are feeding, and use a drag-free drift. Emergences of *S. tibialis* generally take place from 11:00 a.m. until 3:00 p.m. The best populations are found from the Cascade Picnic grounds downstream to Sulphur Cauldron. As with most mayflies we have discussed, the heaviest emergences occur during cool, cloudy weather.

On warm, calm evenings spinners are frequently seen on the water, but they are usually mixed with other species of mayfly so that an exact pattern is not necessary. A small olive spinner (one that also imitates *A. margarita* and *E. inermis*) is effective.

Selected emergence:
    Yellowstone: August 15 - October 1

Mahogany Dun

September is a time of change in West Yellowstone. Gone are the throngs of summer tourists, and the town's summer help has left to go back to school. In Yellowstone Park the animals are beginning to show themselves again; bison are starting to migrate towards winter range, bull elk are bugling and gathering their harems in the meadows, and the green winged teal are no longer seen along the lakes. The weather, which is always capricious, is even more unsettled. One day can be sunny and seventy degrees, the next can be snowy and thirty degrees.

September is also a period of change for the fishing. There are fewer fishermen around and fewer hatches to fish. The fall hatches that do remain, because they are so few in number, become that much more significant. The trout are always looking for good meals, and the fishermen are searching for the corresponding rises of fish. One insect that stimulates some of these last rises is the Mahogany Dun.

Mahogany Duns are mayflies in the genus *Paraleptophlebia* (Para-lep-toe-flee'-bee-uh). The nymphs are three tailed and fair swimmers; their color is varying shades of brown. The duns likewise are three tailed, with a dark gray wing, and, as the name suggests, a mahogany colored body. Both nymphs and adults are typically size #16. Several species of *Paraleptophlebia* emerge throughout the summer, but the fall species, *P. bicornuta* (bye-cor-new'-tuh), and *P. debilis* (duh-bill'-iss) are the most significant. We've found that the earlier summer species are sporadic, and, because of the presence of other more numerous insects, seldom important on their own. The river with the best fishable emergence is the Henry's Fork, but *Paraleptophlebia* are also found in good numbers on the Gallatin River, especially below Squaw Creek. We have occasionally seen small hatches on the Firehole River and Cliff Lake, but these have been isolated experiences.

On the Henry's Fork, *Paraleptophlebia* can be found emerging from August 20th until the end of September. Blanket hatches cannot be expected as a rule, but because the only other insect usually present in good numbers are tiny *Tricorythodes*, the fish will regularly take the larger, less numerous *Paraleptophlebias*.

Rainbows are especially fond of taking the nymphs in the surface film. Unless we specifically find a trout that is taking adults and won't take our nymph, we always fish with a nymph imitation. In fact, a *Paraleptophlebia* nymph is a good fly to fish on the Henry's Fork any time during September, even if there are no naturals around, because the fish relish them. *Paraleptophlebia* generally emerge from mid-morning until early afternoon, and hatches are seldom as heavy as those of other mayflies.

Spinners can be observed in the mornings on the water too, mostly in small numbers, and we haven't encountered a spinner fall yet where a specific imitation was needed.

The less productive, pocket-water of the Gallatin doesn't require specific flies or tactics, since the fish don't have the luxury of allowing food to pass them by. A #14 or #16 Royal Wulff is plenty of fly if you happen to witness an emergence.

Selected emergences:
Henry's Fork: August 20 - September 30
Gallatin: July, September - October

Heptagenia

There are several species of mayfly in the *Heptagenia* (Hep-tuh-gene'-ee-uh) genus found around Yellowstone, but there is only one that can be considered significant to fishermen.

This is *Heptagenia solitaria* (sol-uh-tare'-ee-uh), a late summer mayfly that emerges on the Yellowstone River in the Park. On a year to year basis the emergence can be inconsistent due to dramatic population fluctuations, but when there are adequate numbers of mayflies the fishing is superb.

Superficially, the nymphs of *Heptagenia* resemble those of the Pink Lady. Both are strongly flattened, but *Heptagenia* nymphs have three tails to *Epeorus's* two. The color of *H. solitaria* nymphs is amber, but other species range from translucent gray to medium brown. The bodies of *Heptagenia* nymphs may also be covered with an intricate pattern of black markings.

The duns of *H. solitaria* have two tails, and are gray to grayish-brown in body color. Their wings are a medium gray. The size of the nymphs and duns is #14 to #16. The duns emerge any time from 1:00 p.m. to 5:00 p.m., and our favorite water to find them in is around the Sulphur Cauldron. Though we are always on the lookout for a spinner fall of this species, we have never observed more than a handful of individuals at any one time and consider them insignificant.

The emergences of *H. solitaria* are always concentrated in shallow, slow water along shore. The adults are only seen floating down a ten to twenty foot wide strip along the banks. When we first encountered this behavior it struck us as highly peculiar, for it was something we had never observed with any other mayfly. It wasn't until we visited with Dan Gustafson, an entomologist working for the state of Montana, that the explanation became clear. He noted that it was common for *Heptagenia* nymphs to congregate near shore in slow water prior to emergence, so the emergence behavior we witness is the natural outcome of such migrations.

This knowledge is critical in order to first find and then fish a *H. solitaria* emergence. In September, water levels are low on the Yellowstone, and there are many stretches where the water is ideal for *Heptagenia* emergences. Besides the Sulphur Cauldron area, the water around Buffalo Ford and the stretches above LeHardy Rapids have good emergences. Even the really shallow areas are worth looking over, as we have often observed fish rising in just six inches of water. Though

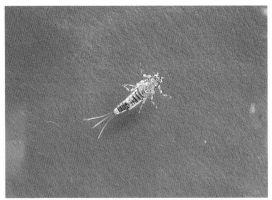

Baetis tricaudatus, nymph

Baetis tricaudatus, male dun

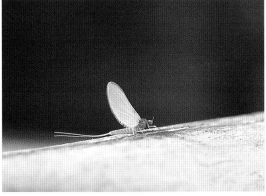

Baetis punctiventris, female dun

Baetis punctiventris, female spinner

Rhithrogena morrisoni, nymph

Rhithrogena morrisoni, female dun

Rhithrogena morrisoni, female spinner

Pale Morning Dun, nymph

Pale Morning Dun, female dun

Pale Morning Dun, male spinner

Green Drake, nymph

Green Drake, female dun

Brown Drake, nymph

Brown Drake, female dun

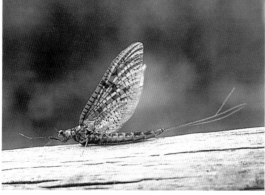

Brown Drake, female spinner

Flav, nymph

Flav, female dun

Flav, female spinner

Gray Drake, nymph

Gray Drake, male dun

Gray Drake, male spinner

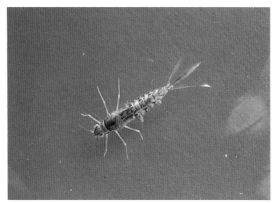

Callibaetis, nymph

Callibaetis, male dun

Callibaetis, female spinner

Tricorythodes, female dun

Tricorythodes, male spinner

Pink Lady, nymph

Pink Lady, female dun

Pink Lady, female spinner

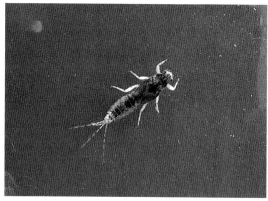

Attenella margarita, nymph

Attenella margarita, female dun

Serratella tibialis, female dun

Serratella tibialis, female spinner

Mahogany Dun, nymph

Mahogany Dun, female dun

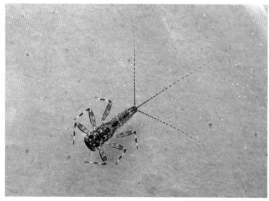

Heptagenia species, nymph

Heptagenia solitaria, female dun

Brachycentrus occidentalis, pupa

Brachycentrus occidentalis

Hydropsyche cockerelli

Helicopsyche borealis

Glossosoma montana

Oecetis disjuncta

Cheumatopsyche lasia

Lepidostoma pluviale

Arctopsyche grandis, larva

Arctopsyche grandis

Hesperophylax designatus

Rhyacophila bifila, larva

Rhyacophila coloradensis

Micrasema bactro

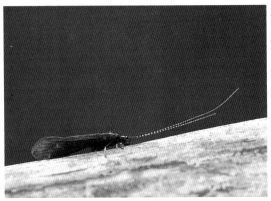

Mystacides alafimbriata

Salmonfly, nymph

Salmonfly, adult

Golden Stone, nymph

Golden Stone, adult

Little Yellow Stone

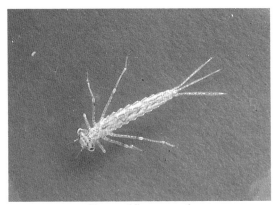

Damselfly, nymph

Damselfly, adult

Midge, adult

the cutthroat are not shy trout to begin with, they are still easily spooked from these spots if you are not careful in your approach and presentation. We usually fish a #16 Sparkle Dun during this emergence, and 6x tippet is mandatory.

The other species of *Heptagenia* in this area are generally only observed as spinners hovering in small swarms over rivers like the Madison, Gallatin and Henry's Fork, during July and August. Even though they are frequently seen, in our experience these beautiful ginger-bodied flies are of no fishing importance.

Selected emergence:
    Yellowstone: August 25 - September 20

Caddisflies

Caddisflies are the insects least understood by fishermen. They are as significant as the mayflies for a Yellowstone fisherman, and a knowledge of basic caddis habits is essential for success during much of the season. It is largely caddis emergences that baffle fishermen, and merely being able to recognize when caddis are hatching is the critical first step in understanding caddis.

In his book *Caddisflies*, Gary LaFontaine notes three signs that indicate when caddis are emerging on rivers, and they are worth repeating. First, trout occasionally are seen leaping in the air. He notes this happens when trout chase emerging caddis pupae; the fish's momentum sometimes carries it right out of the water.

The second clue is that there are no insects on the water. Even during a heavy emergence, adult caddis are just about impossible to see drifting on the surface. They generally emerge and fly off unnoticed. This phenomenon always amazes us. Many times we have held our noses at water level just below a pocket full of trout rising madly to caddis, hoping to see just one adult fly off. Indeed, it is nothing short of a miracle if you do.

Third, LaFontaine writes that most of the feeding trout are bulging and splashing. This occurs as the fish take the pupae from the surface film and turn downward. While this is sometimes true, we find that the riseform is more dependent on the speed of the current the fish is in rather than the food being taken. That is, in fast water bulging and splashing does occur, but in slower water quiet dimples, porpoise rolls, or tails breaking the surface are much more common rise forms. It is important to consider the riseform in deciding what a trout may be taking, but it is wise never to make a judgement based solely on it.

We think that the strongest clue to a caddis hatch, aside from knowing what insects to expect (that's where we hope this book will help), is that no insects are seen on the water, and yet fish are rising. Nine times out of ten that is a dead giveaway that caddis are emerging.

We fish two types of fly during caddis emergences. One is a caddis pupa, the other an emerging caddis pattern. Depending on the species, one type often works better than the other. We make our recommendations under each individual caddis.

Our approach to feeding fish is straight upstream in pocket-water. We prefer to fish our flies dead drift, and this approach avoids casting across a mixture of currents. Fishing downstream and swinging a caddis pupa works, but we think the larger fish prefer taking a dead-drifted fly. It is also possible, and advantageous, to get much closer to rising trout in pocket-water by approaching them from below.

Caddis often emerge best in evening and after dark, and getting close to the fish helps us keep track of our casting when visibility is poor. We often fish with a fixed line length, adjusting *our* position in relation to the fish; that way we know where our fly is at all times.

In smooth water we like to position ourselves to cast across and slightly downstream to rising fish. We are generally a little further from the fish in smooth water, and the down and across angle is best for getting a drag-free drift. Too, this angle keeps you from having to cast the leader over the fish. This is rarely a problem in pocket-water because of the already disturbed surface, but a bad presentation in smoother water often means a spooked trout.

Certain caddis offer fishing opportunities when the females lay their eggs. Egglaying is accomplished by several methods, including bouncing and fluttering along the surface, crawling underneath the water, or floating flush on the surface as a mayfly might. Again, as with an emergence, there are keys to recognizing egglaying activity.

Fly fishermen often think that when caddis are swarming in the air that egglaying, or even an emergence, is taking place. Not true. These flights of caddis (and they can be immense) are usually just swarms of males slowly moving upriver, and there is no correlation between them and egglaying or emergence activities. Egglaying is recognized by watching the water closely for bouncing caddis, finding spent females on the water, or by checking grassy banks, rocks, and logs (or your waders) that protrude from the river. These sites give underwater egglayers access to the water and they often swarm around or congregate on them.

We use a variety of dry patterns to imitate egglaying caddis, and our presentations are always dead-drift. Even though the naturals may display lots of movement our experience shows that the best fish still prefer a dead-drift presentation.

Likewise, if we fish caddis larvae imitations, we do so strictly dead-drift. Naturals are incapable of swimming and completely at the mercy of the currents. Larvae patterns should be weighted and fished along the bottom. We always use floating lines, and if necessary add weight to the leader to keep our flies near the bottom.

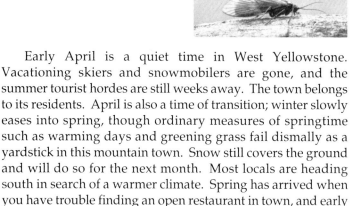

Brachycentrus

Early April is a quiet time in West Yellowstone. Vacationing skiers and snowmobilers are gone, and the summer tourist hordes are still weeks away. The town belongs to its residents. April is also a time of transition; winter slowly eases into spring, though ordinary measures of springtime such as warming days and greening grass fail dismally as a yardstick in this mountain town. Snow still covers the ground and will do so for the next month. Most locals are heading south in search of a warmer climate. Spring has arrived when you have trouble finding an open restaurant in town, and early April is that time. For fishermen it is also time to begin thinking of caddisflies.

Heavy emergences of *Brachycentrus occidentalis* (Brack-ee-sen'-trus ox-uh-den-tay'-lis) begin around the tenth of April on the thermally influenced waters of the Madison and Firehole Rivers in Yellowstone Park. This is the first major caddisfly of the year to emerge on trout streams, and it is fed upon readily by the trout. It is a caddis that exhibits considerable sexual dimorphism in size: the females are a full size #14, the males a #16. Both are a choice meal for fish whose main surface foods until now have been small *Baetis* mayflies and midges. *Brachycentrus* are dark gray in color, almost black at times, and both sexes have distinct olive-hued stripes on the sides of their gray abdomens. These stripes, combined with the time of year they emerge, is a reliable identification feature.

The emergences of *B. occidentalis* on the Madison and Firehole are unique because of the thermal influences in the watershed. *Brachycentrus* is normally an explosive, concentrated emerger, with millions upon millions of individuals emerging over a period of a few days. Instead of these typically quick, mind-boggling emergences, the Park waters experience less intense hatches extended over a much longer period. Fishable numbers can be seen on both rivers from early April until the beginning of July. Yellowstone Park doesn't even open for fishing until Memorial Day weekend, but fishermen can still have a month of *Brachycentrus* activity.

Brachycentrus occidentalis is also referred to as the "Mother's Day caddis", especially in the Livingston and Bozeman areas, where the nearby Yellowstone and Madison Rivers experience incredibly heavy emergences around, coincidentally enough, the holiday of the same name. Sometime around the end of April or early May is the time to expect this activity.

Fishing during the Yellowstone's emergence depends on the spring runoff situation. The yearly appearance of *B. occidentalis* and the beginning of spring runoff frequently coincide. If early May is warm and substantial snowmelt begins, the fishing is usually in jeopardy. The Yellowstone can discolor and rise to the point of unfishablility overnight, ruining some prime early season fishing opportunities. But in those years when the caddis appear a little early, or when snowmelt is delayed by cool weather, the fishing can be phenomenal for both trout and whitefish.

The lower Madison's emergence can be fished more reliably, because runoff usually does not begin before the hatch is well underway. On both these rivers, *Brachycentrus* emerges over a short time period, often lasting barely two weeks, but in much more concentrated numbers than on the Park waters. Both the emergences and the egglaying flights can be spectacular, with seemingly infinite numbers of caddis in the air and on the water. It is not uncommon for huge rafts of spent adults, often inches thick, to build up in back eddies along shore. The best activity is in the afternoon, and the fish will feed readily on both emerging pupae and spent adults. The fish are not difficult to catch, and using a fly that doesn't even resemble *B. occidentalis* is often the best way to compete with a myriad of naturals for a trout's attention. Downwing attractors like the Royal Trude, which are easily visible but still possess a general caddis silhouette, are good choices.

The Henry's Fork at Last Chance, Idaho, is the only other river in the area where emergences of *B. occidentalis* are heavy enough to make it a major insect. The emergence there lasts from May 25th until approximately June 25th. This makes it the first caddis of the year to appear, and aside from *Rhithrogena* mayflies it is the only other sizeable insect present at the end of May.

Most of our fishing on the Madison and Firehole in Yellowstone Park and on the Henry's Fork is done with adult patterns. *Brachycentrus* are most active in the afternoon and evening, and egglaying and emergence often coincide. Egglaying females sprawl awash on the surface or crawl underwater. The underwater egglayers usually resurface, then flop helplessly as they drift downstream. An adult pattern works well whether the fish are taking egglaying adults or freshly emerged caddis. We have rarely run into a situation where the trout feed exclusively on emerging pupae; even when they do, this early in the season it is still possible to fool them with adult patterns.

One other species of *Brachycentrus* is worth mentioning, and that is *americanus* (uh-mare-uh-con'-us). This caddis emerges in August on the Henry's Fork, Yellowstone, and the Madison below Quake Lake. *Brachycentrus americanus* is sparse on the Madison, and we don't consider it a significant caddis there. They are much more important on the Henry's Fork and

Yellowstone, where tremendous numbers are available to the trout. *Brachycentrus americanus* is a lighter gray than *B. occidentalis*, but otherwise both species look similar. Sexual dimorphism is evident in their size too; the females are a #14, the males a #16. Egglaying is the most important stage for fishermen, and this can occur anytime during the day as long as the temperature is fairly cool. Generally in August this means early morning or evening, though a cloudy afternoon is ideal also.

On the Henry's Fork we have cast to fish that were lined up behind protruding rocks and logs, picking off egglaying *B. americanus* as they crawled beneath the surface, laid their eggs, and drifted off with the current. Large numbers of caddis will use these types of site, and the steady flow of naturals is a strong inducement to the fish. Where there are no midstream logs or rocks, the caddis appear to release their eggs at the surface as they hopscotch along.

Selected emergences:
Brachycentrus occidentalis
Madison (YNP), Firehole: April 10 - July 4
Henry's Fork: May 25 - June 25
Madison below Ennis: late April - early May
Yellowstone around Livingston: late April - early May
Brachycentrus americanus
Henry's Fork: August 10 - August 30
Yellowstone: July 25 - August 30

Hydropsyche

The Madison River below Quake Lake appears at first glance to be a large, fast-flowing, continuous riffle. For many fishermen this is a tough sight to reconcile with the classic trout stream, where shallow riffles separate gentle pools in a regular sequence. The Madison is definitely intimidating the first time you fish it, mostly because the eye is drawn to the river's middle, where heavy, turbulent flows crash around huge boulders.

Familiarity breeds understanding though, and as you spend time fishing the Madison you learn to ignore the middle, concentrating instead on the slower pockets along the river's edges. These pockets, which are small and intimate, are where the most fish are caught. Once this is understood the Madison essentially becomes a study in small stream fishing, and its charms are impossible to resist. The Madison flows some forty miles in the section from Quake Lake to the town of Ennis, bisecting a valley of sagebrush covered bench land. Rugged mountains jut from every horizon, and the highest peaks often hold their snow year-round. On pleasant summer evenings, which are frequent, the river is a fly fisherman's paradise.

An angler onstream during evening hours will discover that the air temperature drops considerably from its midday high. As the mercury falls, the strong afternoon winds do likewise. The last of the fluffy cumulus clouds that build up on most afternoons sail off over the Gravelly Range, leaving in their wake a sky so clear and blue and big it could only be Montana. The Madison turns deep blue too, as the day's last rays of light reflect from the water. Insects flying over the surface and the first riseforms are easily spotted in this evening light.

The trout rise sporadically at first, their feeding rhythms perfectly mirroring the insect activity. As darkness sets in the insect activity intensifies and more trout begin to feed. The feeding increases steadily until, at dark, trout are porpoising regularly in every nook, cranny, and hole available. Choosing just one fish to concentrate on is necessary but difficult. You're tempted to cover a different fish if one or two casts go unrewarded, but this tactic is usually futile. Invariably in these situations, the browns and rainbows are feeding on emerging *Hydropsyche* caddis.

The various species of *Hydropsyche* (Hy-dro-sy'-key) are far and away the most important caddis in this area. They are dominant elements in the insect communities of many rivers, and the rises of fish they inspire are Olympian. Of all the stream insects, only the Pale Morning Dun could possibly be more significant.

Heavy *Hydropsyche* emergences occur on local rivers from the middle of May until nearly the end of August. This lengthy schedule results from water temperature variations in the rivers and from that fact at least four separate species of *Hydropsyche* make up this hatch. *Hydropsyche cockerelli* (cocker-ell'-eye) is the first to emerge each year and is the most abundant. *Hydropsyche occidentalis* (ox-uh-den-tay'-lis), *H. oslari* (os'-lair-eye), and *H. placoda* (pla-co'-duh) follow and comprise the rest of the hatch.

All *Hydropsyche* species resemble each other, and they can all be considered synonymous from an imitation and fishing standpoint. Adults come in two sizes; #14 and #16 (the females are usually the larger of the two). Adults have tan wings and bodies of light brown, golden-yellow, or green. The differences in body color are apparent only at emergence; a day or two later the bodies of all species will turn light brown. The wings always remain tan.

Fish will feed heavily on *Hydropsyche* during both emergence and egglaying, but emergence is the major stage. Emergences occur in the evening, and can last for several hours. Their intensity increases as daylight fades, and *Hydropsyche* can be found coming off well past dark.

Egglaying usually occurs sporadically throughout the day, but there are often peaks in the early morning and early evening. The number of egglaying caddis you can expect to see, even during the peaks of their activity, never approaches those found during the emergences.

The larvae of *Hydropsyche* build simple retreats to live in, not true cases like other caddis. They construct nets to seine particles of food from the current. Trout no doubt occasionally feed on larvae accidentally caught in the current, but we feel they are not important enough to warrant specific imitations.

Evening *Hydropsyche* fishing generally follows a predictable pattern. We like to arrive onstream in early evening in case there are female caddis egglaying. Egglaying

Hydropsyche are easy to see because they fly low over the water and are fairly large. These females release their eggs by repeatedly bouncing on the surface or by flopping and twitching as they drift on the surface.

During this egglaying activity, trout will chase the female caddis readily. Aggressive, splashy riseforms are common in these situations, regardless of the size of the fish. This feeding is purely happenstance and opportunistic because the adult caddis are usually scattered widely. Some fish may see many caddis, other fish will see none. We prefer to fish floating adult caddis patterns during this activity and we limit our casting to rising fish. Doing so avoids disturbing too much water.

Frequently in the early evening, male *Hydropsyche* from earlier emergences assemble over the water into mating flights. These caddis flights can completely span a river, and often reach a height of thirty feet. Many fishermen confuse mating flights with a caddis emergence or a caddis egglaying period. They are neither. After flying slowly upriver, these flights of male *Hydropsyche* eventually disperse without ever becoming available to the trout. Even though no fishing results from the flights, it is still an impressive sight to witness.

As evening progresses and the temperature cools, egglaying ceases and emergence begins. The two stages rarely overlap. As trout begin taking emerging *Hydropsyche* pupae, their feeding rhythm and riseforms change. Dorsal fins and tails often break the water surface as the fish take the pupae right beneath the surface. The rises are deliberate and unhurried. Only the small fish rise aggressively now, at times rocketing themselves completely into the air in their efforts to take the pupae.

Though the trout are feeding primarily on pupae, we do not always fish a pupal pattern. The Iris caddis or X-caddis, which imitate an emerging caddis stuck in its shuck, are two of our favorite patterns to use. These patterns are fished dry, and they sometimes seem to work better than strict imitations of the pupae.

Hydropsyche emergences can last well past dark, and the fish will continue to feed as long as there are caddis available. We have found *Hydropsyche* emerging as late as 11:30 p.m. in

July on the Madison River.

On the Firehole River, it appears that the water temperature influences the behavior of *Hydropsyche*. There are spring and fall peaks to the emergence; May, June and October are the best months. *Hydropsyche* is present but sparse and scattered during July, August, and September.

Selected emergences:
  Firehole River: May 15 - October 16
  Henry's Fork: May 20 - June 25
  Madison River: June 5 - August 15
  Yellowstone River: July 10 - August 24

Helicopsyche

These tiny caddis appear in quantity on two Yellowstone area trout streams, the Firehole and Henry's Fork, and they can torment fishermen not prepared to match the small size. They emerge during June and early July, at a time when so many other larger, more noticeable insects are doing likewise that they are easily overlooked. The only species in this genus found here is *Helicopsyche borealis* (Hell-uh-co-sy'-key bore-ee-al'-iss). *Helicopsyche borealis* belongs to a family of caddis that is mostly tropical, warm water oriented, so it is no surprise to find them *en masse* in the Firehole, which regularly reaches temperatures in the low eighties during the middle of summer. Warm water is not a strict requirement however; the Henry's Fork flows much cooler and supports a tremendous population too. There are also populations in some cold spring creeks in the Gallatin Valley.

Helicopsyche borealis is a size #20 caddis, with dark gray wings and a striking amber body. The prime fishing opportunities occur during the female's egglaying activity, but the Firehole and Henry's Fork situations differ enough for us to examine them separately.

The Firehole emergence runs from mid-June until early July, but it would be rare in this time frame to encounter a heavy emergence of these caddis and find fish feeding on them. It can happen, but this is not something to go looking for or planning a day around. On the Firehole *H. borealis* fishing is primarily during egglaying activity, and this action can be found easily if it is sought out. There are four requirements: one, a comfortably cool afternoon or warm evening; two, grassy banks that extend down into the water; three, enough water depth at the bank so fish can feel comfortable coming in close and feeding; and four, current speed slow enough to make it worthwhile for trout to feed on the tiny caddis. If the first three requirements are met but not the fourth, you may see caddis on the water, but you will not see feeding fish. A trout cannot survive expending more energy in the process of feeding than it gains from whatever it is eating! Upper Muleshoe Bend is an example of the right type of water, and there are many others along the entire length of the river.

When conditions are right for egglaying, female *Helicopsyche* ride the water in a ten-foot strip along the banks. They arrive on the water in two ways; most commonly the females simply hop off the grass onto the water, oviposit, and then ride serenely down the river. We have also watched adult females using bankside grass (or our waders if we're dangling our feet in the water) to crawl underneath the surface. After ovipositing underwater, they then release their grip on the substrate and float back to the top. Regardless of how they get there, once on the water there seems to be no further attempt to leave. Also, the spent females are not lying flush in the film like other species might; they drift in the normal resting position their photograph depicts.

Fishing, therefore, is restricted to the banks, and our tactics involve walking the banks looking for risers, wading only when we have spotted a nice fish we want to try. Our approach is from above the fish, casting downstream and back towards the bank. We have had little success fishing upstream in these situations; large Firehole trout in flat water simply won't stand for having a leader cast over their heads. Too, there is invariably some wind present, and it is much easier to adjust your presentation from above, letting your fly drift down over the fish only when you have made a good cast.

On the Henry's Fork it is possible to fish emergences of *Helicopsyche* as well as the spent females. The month of June is ideal, and they frequently emerge in the evening. It is extremely difficult to tell when trout are eating *Helicopsyche* and not one of the other caddis species invariably present. A seine is mandatory, as is a lot of patience in its use. The best clue to *H. borealis* feeding is an overall abundance of them in the seine. And remember, in typical caddis fashion you probably won't see any adults on the water surface during emergence.

Egglaying activity is the same on the Henry's Fork as on the Firehole, and it outweighs the emergences in importance. Water depth is critical here too, as is water speed. You can expect to see tremendous numbers of *H. borealis* on the Henry's Fork, and the fish will definitely come in to shore if there is sufficient water depth. Since the gradient of this river is gentle, finding slow water along shore is no problem, and fish can position themselves along almost any bank. More than once we have seen *Helicopsyche* undermine a Green Drake emergence, with the fish concentrating on the more numerous though markedly smaller caddis and ignoring the Drakes. A correct imitation was invaluable, as was fishing back into the bank from above the fish.

Selected emergences:
    Firehole River: June 10 - July 10
    Henry's Fork: May 28 - July 5

Glossosoma

The species of *Glossosoma* (Gloss-uh-so'-muh) are the smallest caddis in the Yellowstone area that can be of significance to fishermen. These caddis range in size from #20 to #24, with grayish black bodies and wings. They are notable for having an extended emergence span; on the Henry's Fork, for example, we have encountered them from May 31 until September 5. Unfortunately, their importance in fishing is somewhat limited by their tiny size and the fact that they are sporadic emergers.

But *Glossosoma* does have a way of showing up unexpectedly in good numbers, and trout often see fit to dine on them to the exclusion of other, larger insects. The first time they came to our attention on the Madison is a classic example.

We were fishing on a warm July evening and had been fairly successful using imitations of the scattered *Hydropsyche* that were emerging. As darkness set in, the trout picked up the rhythm of their feeding, and we picked up the rhythm of our casting. The situation seemed straightforward enough; darkness was prompting more *Hydropsyche* to emerge, which in turn stimulated the fish to begin feeding more intensely. Strangely enough though, we didn't find ourselves catching any more fish. In fact, we caught fewer. After casting futilely for awhile, changing patterns, and casting some more, we did what we should have done originally—haul out the seine and find out what was going on. (Why do we always have to flail unsuccessfully before we bring out the seine? Why not get it out immediately upon failure and dispense with the fly changes and wasted casting? It occurs to us that we are foolish enough sometimes to think we have this whole thing figured out; we want to believe what our past experiences *have* told us, instead of what the river *is* telling us. Thank goodness nature still delivers a thorough comeuppance now and then to bring us back to reality).

As it always seems to, the seine revealed the unexpected: a large number of *Glossosoma* emergers were mixed in with a smattering of *Hydropsyche* pupae. Another change in flies changed our success, and we landed a couple more fish that evening.

Glossosoma caddis are easily observed in abundance on streamside grasses during their emergence spans, but as we said earlier, they are sporadic, unpredictable emergers. It is impossible to plan on fishing an emergence, but it is advisable to carry a few pupal imitations. We have gone whole seasons on some rivers without needing them, but at other times we've used them frequently. Yearly fluctuations in population density seem pronounced with *Glossosoma*.

During some years there may never be heavy emergences, which could go a long way to explaining our fractured experiences. We have never witnessed any egglaying activity of *Glossosoma* either and conclude for now that it is not important to fishermen. There are several species of *Glossosoma* in this area, but we find mostly *G. montana*.

Selected emergences:
Henry's Fork: May 31 - September 5
Madison River below Hebgen: June 25 - July 30
Firehole River: June 20 - September 21

Oecetis

The Henry's Fork is big water, by most trout stream standards. Big, but deceptive, for there are few places outside the Box Canyon that cannot be waded. The river's consistently wide, meandering span is home to the richest assemblage of important trout stream insects in this area. The river also harbors a population of beautiful rainbow trout that continue, no matter how large they grow, to surface feed on these same insects.

June is often thought of as mayfly time on the Henry's Fork, what with Pale Morning Duns, Green Drakes, Brown Drakes, and others making their yearly appearance. Often neglected, though, are the numerous caddisflies making their appearances too. One of these species is *Oecetis disjuncta* (Ee-see'-tus dis-junk'-tuh).

Oecetis has a very slender, unique profile to its wing, but their most obvious feature is the exceptionally long antennae they sport. *Oecetis* bodies are extremely short relative to their long wings, and exhibit pronounced sexual dimorphism in coloration. Male *O. disjuncta* display a bright blue-green body, and the females have brilliant golden-yellow bodies. Both sexes have light gray wings, and their overall size is #16.

These caddis are most prevalent on the Henry's Fork, but the watchful fisherman will find some on the Gibbon in Yellowstone Park, and a few down on the Madison below Quake Lake. While we have fished the odd emergence, the importance of *Oecetis* is most dramatic during egglaying activity.

Late afternoon and evening is the time to expect both an emergence and egglaying flight. During egglaying, *Oecetis* appear rather suddenly on the water surface, and in numerous positions. They may ride the water in a perfectly normal resting position, they may be found sprawled awash with wings fully spread, or in any position in between. Upside down with two wings tucked in along their bodies and two awash seems to be a favorite posture. Regardless, they make excellent models for spent caddis imitations. Both females and males will be on the water in good numbers.

Last summer, with Ken Takata along for the trip, we pulled up to the bank of the Henry's Fork about 5:30 p.m. on a sunny, warm June afternoon. With the temperature still plenty high we thought we could take our time and rig up casually, since no activity usually begins until things cool down. Wrong. One look at the river revealed a pod of rainbows porpoising avidly. (As we noted earlier, we have always found it a terrible idea to look at the water first before stringing up; if something is happening we find preparing suddenly much more difficult. Despite this, we always give in and take a peek).

Upon entering the water, we discovered spent *Oecetis* already covering the surface. Proper imitations were tied on and we began fishing, eventually covering all available risers. Result: a complete shutout. Though the fish were sipping the spent adults they were also moving around a great deal. We simply couldn't get our flies in front of the fish when and where they decided to rise. Eventually we chased off or put down all the feeding rainbows. As always, there is more to fishing than just matching the hatch, especially on the Henry's Fork.

An important lesson, though, is that fishing the correct fly removes a critical variable, freeing you to concentrate on your approach and presentation, and eliminating worry about whether you should be changing flies. Because *Oecetis* is such a distinctive fly, and fish usually feed on it exclusively, it is an especially good idea to carry imitations in your box if you plan to fish the Henry's Fork. Most other times we have found the fish very approachable and receptive to imitations of *Oecetis*.

While emergences and egglaying flights are sporadic on the Gibbon and Madison, the use of spent *Oecetis* patterns is often highly successful on these rivers. You will probably never see trout feeding exclusively on the naturals, but we wonder if the trout just might remember the distinctive profile of *Oecetis*, and take any opportunity that arises to feed on them.

Selected Emergences:
Henry's Fork: June 10 - June 28
Gibbon: June 20 - July 5
Madison: (sporadic) July 20 - July 30

Cheumatopsyche

Late June is a special time of year in Yellowstone country, carrying with it a promise of abundant hatches, good water conditions, and days filled with rising fish. On cool and overcast mornings, especially when the clouds are the thick, black, low-slung variety that shroud the mountains for the whole day, everyone gets excited. These are conditions that almost assure good insect emergences and good fishing. Enthusiasm rises in the local fly shops on days like these.

Everyone who knows what's up is anxious; guides are upbeat as they plan the day for their clients, knowledgeable fishermen who appreciate how precious these days are thank the fishing gods, and all the fly shop help, ourselves included, jockey for time off. Work shifts are bought, sold, and traded like a commodity, and there is never less respect for a fellow worker than when one of these June days is on the block. Those who have the time off, or who somehow get it, parade it ruthlessly before those who don't.

It was our chance not too long ago, and we had high expectations as we drove down to the Henry's Fork, with Fred Harrison along, for a day's fishing. We arrived about 8:30 a.m., thinking we could take our time and string up casually before the Pale Morning Duns started emerging around mid-morning, as they are wont to do. To our surprise there were fish feeding already, but to what? On such a cold morning, it was too early for Pale Morning Duns or *Baetis* to be active, and there was too much wind for a spinner fall, so we guessed caddis.

After hurriedly stringing our rods, we waded across the river to where the fish were rising and checked the surface. It was caddis, and *Cheumatopsyche* (Key-matt-o-sy'-key) was the genus. *Cheumatopsyche* have a tendency to ride the water for considerable distances after emerging, and combined with the cold weather, they were drifting unusually far that morning. The fish were sipping them regularly and we felt fortunate to be able to work over many nice fish well before the Pale Morning Duns began emerging. We fished adult imitations and landed several rainbows.

Our fishing experience with *Cheumatopsyche* is limited to the Henry's Fork. There are two species we have seen in quantity, *C. pettiti* (pe-tie'-tie) and *C. lasia* (lay'-zhe-uh). Both caddis look alike and can be imitated as one. *Cheumatopsyche pettiti* has a longer emergence span, from roughly June 15 to August 5. *Cheumatopsyche laysia* can be expected during the month of July. These caddis are closely related to *Hydropsyche* and, as can be seen from the color plates, superficially resemble their larger cousins. Their bodies are distinctly olive in color however, and their size is #18. Wing color is tan to medium brown.

Emergence is the only time when we have found *Cheumatopsyche* to be important. The fish will concentrate on the emerging pupae, but seem willing to rise and take adult imitations just as well as they do pupal patterns. Perhaps this is because *Cheumatopsyche*, unlike so many other caddis, will ride the water for a distance after emerging. In fact, this visual clue is the best indication we know that trout may be feeding on them. We have seen emergences take place at all times of the day; the only consistent requirement seems to be reduced light levels (hence our early morning episode above). Emergences are not particularly regular, nor especially heavy, but then it doesn't take too many to interest the fish either.

Cheumatopsyche are generally nocturnal egglayers, and we have not seen an instance where egglaying adults were of consequence. Our observations, which have been as late in the day as 10:30 p.m., have revealed only scattered spent adults on the water surface. We have not found fish feeding on them, but we certainly acknowledge the possibility.

Selected emergence:
 Henry's Fork: June 15 - August 5

Lepidostoma

This caddisfly is widespread in the Yellowstone area, almost as much so as *Hydropsyche*, and while not as abundant as *Hydropsyche*, it is still responsible for some fine fishing. *Lepidostoma* (Lep-uh-duh-sto'-muh) has a long emergence period, and we have enjoyed fishing emergences from the middle of June on the Henry's Fork until early September on the Yellowstone. The species *L. pluviale* (ploo-vee'-al) is the only one of several that is important for fishermen.

Female *Lepidostoma* could be described as the archetypal caddisfly; their wings are an even light brown, their bodies are the classic olive every fisherman associates with caddis, and they run a small #16 to solid #18 in size. The males are a similar brown and olive in color, but also possess a distinctive dark gray recurve on the leading edge of their wings. It is an obvious characteristic and can be seen clearly in the photograph.

Fishing opportunities are available both when *Lepidostoma* are emerging and when they are egglaying. Emergence is generally in the evening, and trout will selectively sip both pupae and adults that are drifting on the surface. The freshly emerged adults sometimes ride the current for ten to twenty seconds, an eternity for most caddis species.

We like to fish pupal patterns because they work better, but an adult fly, which is certainly easier to fish, will catch fish too. Adult patterns fish best when the emergence isn't too heavy; in these instances the fish don't seem to get locked on the emergers so tightly. Regardless of the fly, it should be fished dead drift to individual fish. *Lepidostoma* emergences can be heavy and prompt lots of fish to feed. It is important to single out one fish and work to him, rather than flock shoot. This increases the chance that your fly will float directly over a fish when he is ready to feed. Multiple casts will usually be required if the emergence is heavy.

Our approach to the fish is usually from the side and slightly upstream, except on the Madison. The small pockets on the Madison are best handled by casting straight upstream to the fish. This eliminates many currents that will drag your fly. On larger, smoother water the across and down angle is best for controlling drag.

Both males and females are found riding the water passively during egglaying. Their wings will sometimes be slightly awash in the film, but more frequently *L. pluviale* appears in a normal resting position, with wings folded over their backs. Egglaying activity is heaviest during late afternoon (especially if it's cloudy) and evening, and it is most reliable on the Yellowstone.

How do we know when these caddis are emerging and not egglaying? A seine will tell you right away whether pupae are present, indicating an emergence. But remember, because the adults ride the water after emerging, recognizing what's happening isn't as critical an issue as with other species. An adult imitation is likely to take some fish in either event, which makes *Lepidostoma* one of the easier caddisflies to deal with.

While accompanying some friends on the way to Yellowstone Lake Hotel for dinner one day, we witnessed a great emergence of *L. pluviale*. We had no tackle, but our friends, here on a fishing vacation, had theirs. Since we are all maniacal fishermen, we had to stop and see if we could catch a few of the fish that were working. Our friends strung up, and we recommended tying on a small caddis pupa. Surprise! They had none.

If it had been any other caddis emerging, the situation might have been grim, since the fish would likely have ignored the adults. Not the case here. Our friends tied on small adult caddis and after much ado, hooked a few cutthroat. In such a heavy emergence, a pupa would have been better, but our friends still enjoyed themselves. And we even made it to dinner—several hours later, of course.

Selected emergences:
    Henry's Fork: June 15 - July 10
    Yellowstone: July 22 - September 4
    Madison: July 15 - August 20
    Slough Creek: July 10 - August 20

Arctopsyche

The Gallatin River is an unusual piece of water for this area. It starts as a tiny, cold, mountain stream untouched by man and then grows into a moderately warm, easy-flowing, big river as it spills onto its flood plain prior to entering the Missouri River. This transformation takes place in a brief ninety miles, with no unnatural interruptions, and with most of it occurring in plain view along a major highway. There are trout throughout its length, at least when the valley farmers don't completely dewater the lower end to satisfy their irrigation needs.

Classic pocket-water abounds in the upstream reaches in Yellowstone Park, perfect for prospecting with dry fly or nymph on a warm summer afternoon. Below Big Sky it gains size, and changes to a predictable pool, riffle, pool sequence until it passes Gallatin Gateway. Below there, and continuing north of Bozeman, the river slows some and becomes highly braided. The resultant channels are always in a state of flux; formed and altered by a combination of runoff, seasonal water flows, and irrigation needs.

Substantial elevation is lost in the river's progress downstream, and as the nature of the water changes, so too does its insect community. Dan Gustafson, who spent several years completing a doctoral study of the Gallatin's insects, found that 58 species of mayfly, 67 species of stonefly, and 97 different caddis called the river home; an incredible testament to the Gallatin's diversity. One of the caddis, *Arctopsyche grandis* (Arc-toe-sy'-key gran'-diss), is worth knowing about for fishing purposes.

Arctopsyche is an abundant, large caddis, size #8 to #10, and as a larva is free-living—that is, it does not build protective cases like so many other species. Their body color ranges from a brownish-olive in the Gallatin to a bright olive in the Madison, another river with excellent populations of this caddis. In response to changing water levels and to eliminate crowding as they grow, *Arctopsyche* larvae move about the bottoms of rivers. Because of this movement and their large size, we suspect many are dislodged by the currents and fall prey to trout and whitefish. If the success of big caddis larva patterns is any indication, we can guarantee that trout know what they are and prey readily on these larvae whenever possible. *Arctopsyche* is found in quantity all along the Gallatin, but relative to other insect species seems more important in the Park stretches, perhaps because there are fewer other large insects there. On this river we feel the larval stage is the one to be concerned with; adults are nocturnal and rarely turn out in large numbers.

Adults can occasionally be seen scampering rapidly over streamside rocks on cloudy afternoons or just at dark. We are not sure of their emergence patterns or egglaying behavior, and aside from being used as a model for a large, searching dry fly, we feel they aren't significant in the adult stage on the Gallatin.

The Madison holds large populations of *A. grandi*s from immediately below Quake Lake downstream to roughly McAtee Bridge. We always observe the greatest numbers in the first few miles below Quake. As on the Gallatin, larval imitations are always an excellent fly for blind fishing; whether the fish are actually taking our flies as imitations of *Arctopsyche* we'll never know, but they certainly work. We assume the fish see many naturals drift their way and that they learn to recognize them as a nice meal.

Unlike the Gallatin, it is common during *Arctopsyche's* emergence span to see many adults on the banks of the Madison. They prefer to be active after dark, but will come out on a heavily overcast afternoon. Their behavior typically involves running madly and indiscriminately (at least it seems indiscriminate to us) over streamside rocks, covering lots of ground but not going anywhere. Judging from the large numbers of individuals, you would assume that emergences or egglaying flights would be of great significance, but it isn't so in our experience.

Arctopsyche grandis is largely nocturnal, and we're not sure how important their emergence and egglaying activities are. While we have caught trout on pupal and adult patterns, we have never seen a period where the trout fed exclusively on either stage.

Since this is the largest caddis that emerges in quantity on the Madison, it is still worth imitating in both the adult and larval stages. As we have already said, both are excellent searching patterns to use when no other insect activity is evident.

Selected emergences:
    Gallatin: July
    Madison: June 20 - July 25

Hesperophylax

Hayden Valley is small, as western valleys go, and it lacks the classic, rugged mountain scenery found in so many others. To the casual observer its look is austere, but the landscape is deceptive. Gently rolling sagebrush hills can mask hundreds of grazing buffalo, a wandering grizzly bear, or a cow and calf moose. Herds of elk often remain unseen from visitors anchored by automobile to the valley's single road. And, of course, there is the Yellowstone River. The river's smooth, powerful currents are home to waterfowl of all types, and, underneath, a magnificent trout fishery. It is a valley rich in life, and anything but plain to those who know where to look.

On one late July trip, we headed for the river with Doug Newton. Doug was interested in photographing a moose that had been hanging around the Yellowstone's junction with Alum Creek, so we left town before sunrise. Luck was with us; the moose appeared on schedule and the photo session was over in no time. We continued driving upstream to LeHardy Rapids, and arrived just after 8:00 a.m. Doug immediately jumped out and went to inspect the river.

A minute later he was back, and announced that there were a lot of golden stoneflies both on the water and buzzing over it. Strange, we thought, for stoneflies to be active so early in the morning, so we walked over for a look ourselves. Right away we knew it was the color and size of the flying insects that led Doug to think golden stonefly; in reality he was watching *Hesperophylax* (Hes-per-o-fy'-lax) caddis.

These giant caddis are striking in appearance. Black and white stripes divide each golden-ginger wing, and their bodies are a bright olive. *Hesperophylax* are a full size #8, and when flying at a distance they are easily mistaken for stoneflies. Next to *Arctopsyche, Hesperophylax* is the largest caddis that we consider in this book, and when they get on the water they inspire much consideration from the trout too. *Hesperophylax* is most important on the Yellowstone, but widely scattered individuals will also be seen on the Henry's Fork and the Gallatin. In our experience they do not constitute a significant hatch on either of these two rivers. The important species on the Yellowstone is *H. designatus* (des-ig-nay'-tus).

Because the Yellowstone's opening date for fishing is July 15, we occasionally miss this emergence, or at least a substantial part of it. *Hesperophylax* begins emerging early in July when we have a normal season, and in these instances we are lucky to catch the tail end of it as the fishing season opens. When spring comes late to Yellowstone, scattered *Hesperophylax* can still be found in early August.

Hesperophylax will be taken by trout any time they are on the water, but egglaying periods are when you'll encounter the best concentrations. And by "best concentrations" we mean quantities that number in the low hundreds at most. *H.*

designatus is not as abundant as other caddis species, but their size alone makes them important: fish know what they are and will go out of their way to take them. The adult caddis prefer to congregate along stretches of river where the banks are heavily lined with trees down to the water's edge. During oviposition, *Hesperophylax* tend to drift close to the banks, so it pays to watch for trout that have been lured in close to feed on the naturals. Egglaying can occur anytime from late morning through afternoon.

Since the cutthroat are not particularly selective in the first couple of weeks of the season, almost any large caddis or small golden stonefly pattern will suffice as an imitation when naturals are present. In fact, aside from the fact that trout are fairly opportunistic anyway, one of the reasons many fishermen do so well during these first weeks is that they are unwittingly imitating *Hesperophylax* by the use of large flies and a dragging drift. Egglaying naturals often scuttle around the surface of the water, so occasional drag can work to your advantage, especially in faster water.

Selected emergence:
Yellowstone: July 15 - August 5

Rhyacophila

Of the caddis we cover in this book, this is the only genus whose larvae could be said to truly overshadow the adults in importance to fishermen. This anomaly is due in part to the primitive nature of *Rhyacophila* (Rhy-uh-co'-fil-uh). The ability to build a protective case is a measure of evolutionary advancement in caddisflies, and this feature is absent in this genus. *Rhyacophila* larvae range freely over the bottom of riffles, unencumbered by the stick or stone cases exhibited by most of their relatives.

Primitive caddisflies generally thrive in cold, highly oxygenated water; rivers like the Gallatin and the Madison below Quake Lake are excellent habitat, and both rivers host large populations of many *Rhyacophila* species. An exception to this rule is the Firehole River in Yellowstone Park, which also has a fine population despite a much warmer temperature.

The larvae of the important species in this area are a bright, intense green in color, well known as "caddis green" to most fishermen. There is no doubt that trout and whitefish recognize these shades of green, and imitations of *Rhyacophila* larvae are among the best choice of fly to fish in the rivers where they are found. We also think that the success of so many different green nymph patterns is a consequence of fish mistaking them for natural *Rhyacophila* larvae.

In fact, one could argue these imitations are the most useful searching patterns, period, on the Madison or Gallatin. Since the natural larvae are present in mature form from June well into October, and since the larvae occur often in the natural drift of a stream, fish are given a multitude of chances to prey on them. Though the same thing can be said of several stoneflies, fish are far more willing to take smaller caddis imitations in the middle of summer with water levels down. This shyness towards larger imitations in the summer is a curious fact, and we wonder if the fish also shy away from larger naturals, such as stonefly nymphs. It seems unlikely they would pass up a large natural nymph, but they definitely avoid large imitations. Why this is so we can only speculate, but it makes the smaller caddis larvae imitations more valuable flies.

The two most important species of *Rhyacophila* are *R. bifila* (bye-fee'-luh) and *R. coloradensis* (col-lar-uh-den'-sis). *R.bifila* is found emerging earlier in the year, from July through August, and *R. coloradensis* is found from roughly mid-September until the end of October. As we noted earlier, the larvae of both species are an intense green, often with small areas of darker olive. Their heads are generally black or various shades of brown. Size runs from #14 to #16, and the larvae are found in turbulent pocket-water.

The adults of both species also resemble each other, with beautifully speckled gray and black wings and olive bodies. They too range in size from #14 to #16. Their importance in fishing is not great. While the adults are easily observed in exceptional quantities on bankside grass or bridge pilings, we have never witnessed an emergence of consequence. Our experience contradicts that of Gary LaFontaine, who writes in his fine book *Caddisflies*, "In the rapids on the Madison River below Quake Lake [*R. bifila*] emerges in good numbers every evening during July". If they are emerging in good numbers, they do not do so in a well coordinated manner, and they do not elicit any particular response from the trout.

July on the Madison is *Hydropsyche* time, and it is the emergence of these caddis, not *Rhyacophila*, that power the tremendous rises of trout in the evenings. When we have seined below pods of rising trout, we have never found *Rhyacophila* to be more than a token presence, if present at all. Perhaps *R. bifila* is emerging heavily at some time of the day, but we believe their emergences are sporadic and therefore completely overshadowed by the concentrated emergences of *Hydropsyche*.

The autumn emergences of *R. coloradensis* are similar to those in the summer. The adults can be seen in number on the banks, bridges, etc., but cannot be found emerging *en masse*. The concurrent fall *Baetis* emergences are infinitely more important to the fishermen.

During September and October on the Firehole, we have seen good numbers of *R. coloradensis* laying eggs on the water surface. The fish will feed readily on these ovipositing caddis. Some caddis will float calmly, others hopscotch over the surface, so it is not unusual to see both quiet and violent rises from fish feeding on the same insect. Most of the time only the smaller fish rise exuberantly; the larger fish are content to take the quietly drifting caddis, and they do so calmly. This egglaying activity on the Firehole is the only situation we have encountered where an adult imitation is required.

These egglaying *Rhyacophila* are usually found in the riffles on the Firehole. The water from Fountain Flat Drive upstream past Ojo Caliente Springs is ideal habitat. Look for rising trout in the riffles and immediately below them, where the water smooths out into pools.

Both our larval and adult imitations are fished dead drift. Remember that the larval patterns are important searching flies to use during those times when no insect emergences are taking place. In pocket-water, which is where these patterns should be fished, we fish upstream. Our larval patterns are weighted so that they drift near the bottom, where trout expect to see them. Occasionally it is necessary to add split shot to keep the fly down. Fishing upstream is the easiest way to maintain a drag-free drift, it is less likely to spook fish, and it allows a strike to be detected quickly.

Selected emergences:
> *Rhyacophila bifila*
> Madison River: July 1 - August 25
> Yellowstone: August 15 - August 30
> Gallatin: July.
> *Rhyacophila coloradensis*
> Madison River: September 5 - October 22
> Firehole: September 15 - October 25

Micrasema

The Yellowstone River in the Park is an exceptionally rich trout fishery, and it is home to yet another important caddisfly, *Micrasema bactro* (My-cruh-seem'-uh back'-tro). This caddis resembles a miniature *Brachycentrus* (the two genera are related) and can be found emerging and egglaying on the silky smooth Yellowstone flats on pleasant summer evenings.

The emergence period for *Micrasema* runs from July 15 through August 8, but they are usually seen for just five to seven days within this three week span. It is an extremely synchronized caddis, with most individuals emerging and egglaying in well coordinated hordes. There are few stragglers, so when the first individuals are observed either emerging or flying upriver, it's a lock that many more will follow promptly. On the evenings they choose to be active there is no question they will be the most abundant, significant insect, and this on a river famous for spewing tremendous numbers of other bugs at this same time.

Micrasema sports black wings that hide a bright green body, and it runs a small #18 to large #20 in size. The Yellowstone cutthroat relish them, both during emergence and oviposition. When they are present the fish often feed on them to the exclusion of other larger flies. Their small stature can present many problems in fishing, chief among them simply recognizing when an emergence is in progress. As with most caddis, adult *Micrasema* do not dawdle on the surface, so you absolutely cannot count on seeing them riding along on the currents. Earlier we mentioned that the combination of rising fish and a lack of obvious insects on the surface usually indicates a caddis emergence, so it's probably tempting to assume these clues could aid the problem.

Elsewhere perhaps, but on the Yellowstone, not a chance. This river is so rich in insect life that we guarantee other insects will be present in good numbers, either emerging or egglaying, so immediately concluding that caddis is the answer is not the best plan of attack. Faced with this situation, and knowing the wide variety of insects that the trout could be feeding on, we've found that immediate and judicious use of the seine has been our best recourse. We know that this is an agonizing task when surrounded by dozens of rising trout, so we won't blame you for wasting time trying an assortment of different flies first. Just remember, we told you to get the seine out.

Analyzing the riseform for an answer is likely to lead nowhere also, because there are at least eight other insects that could be responsible for the same porpoising type rise. So why not try *Micrasema* imitations first? Because the odds are against it; there may only be five or six emergences in a three week period, compared to almost daily hatches of *Hydropsyche* and other flies.

Consequently, if any *Micrasema* do show themselves in the

seine, we immediately tie on and try an appropriate pupal pattern. Simply knowing that they are present and that during emergences they usually outnumber other insects is the best indication that the trout might be feeding on them.

Fortunately, the egglaying activity is much easier to decipher. If you are standing in the river, take a look at your legs; *Micrasema* will utilize them as an egglaying site. The adults land on your waders just above the water level, then crawl under the surface where they paste a sticky green ball of eggs to your boots and lower legs. The ultimate clue that any rising fish are feeding on the egglayers will be when you feel something bumping your leg; look down, and you'll see several cutthroat picking caddis from your waders. It happens, and could only happen, on the wonderful upper Yellowstone.

Most of the fish feeding during egglaying will be taking the spent females after they have laid their eggs and have drifted back to the surface. The females never quite regain the actual surface, but float in the surface film and just below it. A flush floating imitation fished dead drift is deadly.

Though the chances of meeting a *Micrasema* situation may not be as great as for other flies, it is imperative to carry their imitations, for the Yellowstone cutthroat will be extremely selective to them. They will not be the same foolish fish that they were earlier in the season, or even in the same day. The difficulty of capturing one commands our respect. Episodes such as these keep an angler thinking, guessing, and hoping, and they ultimately provide and sustain our fascination for the Yellowstone.

Selected emergence:
    Yellowstone River: July 15 - August 8

Mystacides

On many trout streams, August is a month when aquatic insect activity slows considerably. To maintain steady hatches through this time a stream must be exceptionally diverse, capable of supporting a wide range of insects that can coexist in space and time as well as occupy all types of habitat. Streams this diverse are rare, but the Henry's Fork is one of them.

Diverse habitat is just one of the charms of the Henry's Fork. It has everything from the swiftest, rubble bottomed rapids to silty, meandering, meadow stretches. Slow water, silty bottomed reaches, such as that found in the middle of the Railroad Ranch, support numerous insects adapted specifically to this habitat. August is a time to find *Tricorythodes*, *Callibaetis*, and *Paraleptophlebia* mayflies emerging, and caddis such as *Mystacides alafimbriata* (Mist-uh-see'-dees al-uh-fim-bree-ah'-ta).

Mystacides is a black winged caddis, about a size #16, with a dark gray to black or dull amber body. They have long antennae, much like *Oecetis*, and a similarly low-winged profile. These caddis are primarily active in the early morning hours, from 7:00 a.m. until roughly 10:00 a.m., before the heat of the sun warms the air and drives them to the bankside grasses. During these early August mornings *Mystacides* adults can usually be seen hovering in a dizzying dance a few feet above the river banks. These dancing adults are not necessarily a sign of activity to come; there may or may not be an emergence or egglaying flight. The dance is just a constant reminder to fishermen that caddis are around, and that we should keep them in mind.

Mystacides adults are frequently seen on the water close to the banks, and we believe these are mostly egglaying females. If the water is at an adequate level, trout will come in and sip these adults eagerly. *Mystacides* is seen out on the middle of the river too, but it is difficult to tell whether these are emerging or egglaying. In *Caddisflies*, Gary LaFontaine contends that *Mystacides* pupae crawl out of the water in the mornings to emerge and that the adults dive under the water surface at dusk to lay eggs. Neither of these descriptions quite coincides with our experiences.

At any rate, however these caddis arrive on the water surface, the important factor for fishing is their behavior. *Mystacides* always ride the water calmly in a resting position for considerable distances, which makes them very available to the fish. In typical fashion for these slow water stretches, the rainbows will feed regularly, but between rises they will constantly change their positions. Sometimes it seems as if they are moving to find more caddis, other times it's as if to avoid being cast over. We frequently end up chasing them all over the river, hoping to put just one cast in front of their noses. If a feeding trout can be pinned against a bank, limiting his options to moving only up or down, your chances of raising him improve.

We have always fished adult patterns for *Mystacides*, and have found them to be all that is required. Our friend Paul Brown has had success with soft hackles tied with Starling feathers, fishing them in the film to working fish.

As with all aquatic insects, population fluctuations are common in *Mystacides* and in some years these caddis are more important than others.

Selected emergence:
    Henry's Fork: July 20 - August 30

Notes on stillwater caddis:

Though most of this region's caddis fishing takes place on rivers, there are good caddis populations in some of the lakes too. Unfortunately, we know of no one with a thorough knowledge of the fishing opportunities presented by these lake caddis species.

Our own experiences are fragmented, but may help if you are interested in tracking down some of these caddis. The lake caddis we have encountered are usually members of the family *Limnephilidae* (Lim-nuh-fil'-uh-dee). This is a highly diverse group, with many, many species. Those we've encountered are large in size (#4 - #8 typically) and very active. They skitter quickly across the surface during emergence and egglaying, often inciting the fish into hectic chases and slashing rises.

Virtually all the lakes in this area contain caddis, but the best activity we have experienced has been on Grebe and Hebgen. Woody Wimberly has often brought us samples of the beautiful *Phryganea* (Fra-gay'-nee-uh) caddis from Lewis Lake, along with stories of excellent fishing when they were on the water.

July and August are the months when lake caddis are most active, and calm, warm evenings are likely to provide the best fishing. We use either caddis pupa or adult patterns. If fish are visibly working we cast in front of them and strip our flies back across their path. Depending on how regularly the fish are rising, it's sometimes necessary to guess in which direction the fish are traveling.

Blind casting and stripping can yield surprising results at times too, especially if trout are only occasionally showing themselves on the surface.

Stoneflies

Salmonfly

No other insect creates as much excitement among anglers year after year as does the Salmonfly. All motels in the area are full, fishing guide services are swamped, and drift-boat accesses along the rivers look like flea market parking lots. Fishermen from all over the world assemble to follow and fish "the hatch".

Unfortunately, four out of five years the fishing doesn't live up to all the expectations and hype. Spring runoff, rain, or sporadic concentrations of Salmonflies often combine to produce disappointing angling, and many a float trip has been saved by the more reliable caddisfly emergences. This however, never dampens an angler's spirits and hopes, for hitting that one year in five makes it all worthwhile.

The Salmonfly, *Pteronarcys californica* (Tare-uh-nar'-sis cal-uh-for'-nuh-kuh), is the largest stonefly to emerge from our rivers. Mature nymphs and adults approach three inches in length. Mature nymphs, which are two to four years old, are chocolate brown to black in color. Their bellies turn a distinct orangish prior to emergence.

Adult Salmonflies are unmistakable; their sheer size and orange markings are unlike those of any other insect. Their two pairs of amber wings have pronounced black venation.

Salmonfly nymphs crawl out of the water to emerge. Rocks, bushes, and bridge abutments are all favorite sites and will be covered with empty shucks as the nymphs complete their final molt. Several days prior to emergence, the huge nymphs migrate toward shore in preparation for leaving the water.

But a river's entire Salmonfly population does not emerge at the same time. They begin emerging from the furthest point downstream and the hatch works its way upriver, moving three to four (and sometimes more) miles a day. Adult females return to the water several days later to lay their eggs. Swarms of females fly upstream over the river, bouncing and fluttering on the surface to release their egg masses.

Several strategies can be used to fish the Salmonfly hatch. Nymph fishing ahead of the emergence is especially effective, as the trout and whitefish are on the lookout for migrating nymphs. This is perhaps the most reliable fishing during this hatch and, sometimes, the *only* fishing to be had if the water is off-color.

We fish our nymphs upstream, dead drift. Our leaders are short and stout; 1X tippet is not too heavy. Both fly and leader are weighted enough so that we are fishing on the bottom, where the fish expect to see the naturals. Also, we avoid wading whenever possible. This eliminates spooking the many fish that move in close to shore to feed on the naturals.

Prime dry fly fishing takes place when the female Salmonflies return to the river to lay their eggs. Egglaying usually occurs in the afternoon and early evening. Just like the actual emergence, egglaying flights move upstream each day too. Finding the spot where the females are swarming is critical to dry fly fishing. If you fish upstream of the flights the fish won't be tuned in to the adults yet; downstream the fish are likely to be stuffed and uninterested in feeding.

Locating the right spot is best accomplished by floating the river. This enables you to cover long stretches of water, increasing the odds of finding the egglaying flights and surface feeding fish.

Weather influences Salmonfly flights tremendously. Ideal conditions are sunny, warm, windy days. Salmonflies are clumsy fliers, and brisk winds often knock the adults to the water prematurely and keep them skittering on the surface for longer periods.

Trout frequently display suspicion of adult Salmonflies. The sheer size of the naturals and the fact that they are floating appears to unnerve the fish. Refusals are common; we have seen trout bump our flies, follow them downstream, slap at them and drown them, all without actually taking. Sometimes it seems like the fish are waiting for the fly to move, and twitching your imitation often elicits an instant take.

An undersized fly often succeeds in drawing rises much better than one tied to the exact size of the naturals. Too, a sunken adult imitation occasionally out fishes the floating fly. Trout generally seem more comfortable feeding on these huge creatures underwater than on top, but it is much more fun to fish dry.

We always employ the whole range of tactics: fishing floating patterns dead drift, imparting movement, casting sunken flies. Flexibility is important; don't get caught sticking to one method if it isn't working. There's no telling what tactic may take fish on a given day, and anything's fair game (except, perhaps, dynamite).

As we noted above, fishing immediately downstream of the point of egglaying is frequently a bust. We aren't sure of the exact reason; whether the fish are indeed stuffed and for that reason uninterested is just speculation. But if you get downstream far enough (and there is no set guideline for what "far enough" is), trout can be taken on adult imitations again. In these stretches fish can be caught on adult patterns for up to a week after the actual egglaying flights have passed.

When all is said and done, the Salmonfly hatch can be anything: exciting, frustrating, astonishing, disappointing, or any combination thereof. If the chase somehow doesn't seem worth it, you simply haven't caught that one year in five.

Selected emergences:
    Henry's Fork: late May - early June
    Firehole Canyon: early June
    Madison: late June - early July
    Gallatin: late June - early July
    Yellowstone: July

Golden Stone

Among all stoneflies, the best fishing opportunities are usually presented by the Golden Stones. They are abundant in many rivers and are taken well by fish in both the nymph and adult stage. Golden Stones also tend to be available as adults for longer periods than, say, the Salmonfly.

The major species of Golden Stone in this area is *Hesperoperla pacifica* (Hes-per-o-per'-luh pa-sif'-uh-kuh). As nymphs *H. pacifica* are striking in appearance. They are large in size and feature an array of intricate and beautiful markings, rich in shades of brown and yellow. This species takes three or four years to complete its life cycle, which means there are always nymphs present in a range of sizes. Mature nymphs run in size from #2 - #6, not quite as large as a Salmonfly nymph can be, but still a nice meal for a trout.

Adult *H. pacifica* are, as their name implies, golden in color. Like most insects their color can vary somewhat, but a Golden Stone is not likely to be confused with other flies. The size of the adults ranges from #4 - #8.

Hesperoperla pacifica generally emerges after the Salmonfly, though it is not unusual for them to be seen together as the Salmonfly emergence wanes and the Goldens begin. The nymphs crawl out of the water to emerge, but are not available to the fish until they lay their eggs. Egglaying flights take place in the late morning or afternoon, with the females skittering and hopscotching along the surface of the river.

Golden Stones may not be as numerous as Salmonflies, but they often provide better fishing. Perhaps because of their smaller size trout take the Goldens better than Salmonflies when they are on the surface. We will never forget a late July float we took on the Madison, from Schumaker Ditch to Ennis, with Nick Lyons and his son, Paul. Nick stuck with an adult Golden Stone the entire float, while Paul fished a Golden nymph. Nick took many nice brown trout that day; Paul did equally well, but caught primarily rainbows.

As we mentioned, the Goldens also tend to be around longer than other large stoneflies. On the Yellowstone River in the Park, Golden Stoneflies can be found fluttering around stretches of fast water for a full two months. During those periods no other surface feeding is apparent, blind fishing a Golden Stone adult can always be counted on to raise fish in the riffles. This is true not only on the Yellowstone, but also on rivers like the Gallatin, Gardner, Henry's Fork, and Madison.

Our fishing strategies are the same as for the Salmonfly, with different flies of course.

Selected emergences:
Henry's Fork: July
Madison: early July - mid-July
Gallatin: late June - mid-July
Yellowstone: July - August

Little Yellow Stoneflies

Several species of these yellow stoneflies appear each summer on local rivers, but their importance in fishing is not well understood. While the adults can be seen in good numbers drifting on the water, trout feed on them only in a haphazard way, if at all. We have never witnessed a steady rise of fish to these stoneflies, though many trout can be caught by blind fishing these imitations throughout the day.

The Firehole River and the Madison below Quake Lake are the two rivers where these little stoneflies are most obvious. On the Firehole there is a species of *Isoperla* (Eye-so-purr'-luh) present in June. On the Madison, *Suwallia pallidula* (Sue-wall'-ee-uh pal-uh-due'-luh) can be found on streamside brush during July and August. Both species are available to trout primarily during the egglaying activities of the females. The *Isoperla* species is roughly a size #10, with spots of bright red color on an otherwise yellow abdomen. The females are easily observed flying over the Firehole on warm June afternoons or evenings. After they arrive on the water most drift peacefully downstream, untouched by trout. Sporadic rises are often seen, but we feel these rises are mostly due to the odd caddis or mayfly floating by.

Suwallia pallidula are small stoneflies, size #16 - #18, with beautiful bright yellow bodies and jet black eyes. Prior to sunset on nice July and August evenings, swarms of *S. pallidula* are frequently seen hovering over the Madison River. After these mating flights spent females are a common sight on the river surface, but, just like the Firehole, few trout seem interested. The odd rises that are seen could easily be to the caddis that typically begin emerging about this same time.

Our friend Paris Molinero has spent a lot of time on the small channels of the Madison around Ennis, and he relates stories of regularly catching many fish on imitations of these little stoneflies during July and August evenings. He tells us he never sees rising fish taking these stoneflies either, despite good numbers of naturals on the water.

Our suspicion is that since most of the flies tied to represent these little stoneflies could also pass as a caddis, the trout probably are taking them for a caddis. Nevertheless, it is a good idea to carry a few imitations with you. Even though the fish may take them for a caddis, the success of these flies is still remarkable.

Selected emergences:
    Firehole: June
    Madison: July - mid-August
    Gallatin: July - August

Damselflies

Damselflies are to lake fishing what the Pale Morning Dun is to river fishing: one of the most important insects for both fish and fishermen. Damselflies thrive in almost all the stillwaters in Yellowstone country, from the largest lakes to the tiniest ponds. Even the Firehole River has an exceptional population. On Henry's Lake, just across the Idaho border, fishermen converge from all over the country in early July just to fish the damselfly emergence.

Many species of damselfly live in this area, but because their behavior is similar they can all be treated as one by fishermen (thank goodness). Damselfly nymphs are far more important than the adults because of their greater availability to trout.

The nymphs are long and slender, and they are poor swimmers. They often ambush their prey and are beautifully camouflaged to blend in with natural vegetation. Brown, olive, and green are their dominant colors, and mature nymphs are size #6 -#10. Damselflies emerge by crawling out of the water and completing a final molt. Most nymphs crawl out on shore, but anything that protrudes from the water (rocks, logs, plants, a fisherman's float tube) is fair game as an emergence site.

A heavy emergence is a true spectacle, as wave after wave of these camouflaged creatures march from the water. It always reminds us of some Armed Forces unit storming a beach; the damselflies are like miniature soldiers singlemindedly pursuing their mission of emergence. No matter how many times you pick them up and throw them back in the water they still right themselves, swim to shore, and march out again.

Damselfly nymphs often must expose themselves in the

journey from their weedbed homes to the shoreline. They are terribly ineffective swimmers, moving slowly but steadily via exaggerated side to side undulations of their bodies. The nymphs are extremely vulnerable during these migrations, and trout prey ruthlessly on them.

Damselflies swim to shore at all depths, and trout can be found taking them from the surface film all the way to the bottom. Fishing from a boat or float tube with a sinking line in deep water is an excellent tactic; retrieve your fly in short, steady strips. We especially like to wade the shorelines of lakes, fishing the shallows with floating lines, often to visible fish.

The west side of Henry's Lake is a favorite place of ours. On a sunny day in July the migrating damselflies lure lots of nice trout onto the shallow flats. The trout cruise back and forth and back and forth as they visibly gorge on the nymphs. Often the fish feed at the surface, just like a gulper on Hebgen Lake. The first time we saw this we figured we were about to have a field day.

Unfortunately, it didn't work out that way. The cruising fish were incredibly difficult, ignoring our flies completely for several hours. What seemed so straightforward was not. For one thing, we had no unweighted nymphs, so the surface feeders were untouchable. We concentrated on the fish feeding near bottom but couldn't take them either. Was it our flies? Our presentation? We weren't really sure. In the end one fish was caught, a gorgeous five-pound cutthroat. Still, it was small consolation considering how actively the fish fed.

Lin Tureman, who spends as much time fishing damselfly emergences as anyone, gave us a tip that improved our fishing tremendously. He noted that emerging damselfly nymphs always swim a line perpendicular to the shore, and that the fish are accustomed to seeing them do so. If your fly is not following the same line the naturals are, it is likely to be ignored. We realized that we had been spraying casts at all angles into the water, and during our retrieves our flies were not always on the most direct line possible towards shore.

Even if the flies are not using the shoreline to emerge they still travel directly toward whatever site they have chosen. The angle of retrieve is not a widely considered point by fishermen, but is important when the fishing is difficult.

Adult damselflies are generally not available to trout except during unusual circumstances, such as windy weather, or perhaps while mating. Trout do take the adults whenever they can. We have watched fish along grassy banks on the Firehole jump clear of the water while pursuing adult damsels. And every summer Grebe Lake in Yellowstone Park seems to have several days of excellent adult damsel fishing.

July is the peak month of damselfly activity. Henry's Lake has the best known emergence, but anyone given to exploring other lakes would do well to have damselfly imitations along at all times. Many other lakes (Cliff, Wade, and Grebe come to mind) have fishable populations too.

Selected emergence:
    Henry's Lake: July

Midges

It seems that wherever trout can be found, so too can midges. On all Yellowstone waters midges are an important food source for trout. But their importance is often overlooked by fishermen concentrating on emergences of other, larger insects.

When we are talking about midges we are referring to members of the family *Chironomidae* (Ky-roe-nom'-uh-dee). These two-winged flies come in all sizes, from the huge, #10 - #12 early season midges on Hebgen Lake to the tiny #26 green midges found on the Yellowstone in August. They are most important to fishermen during emergence, when the fish feed heavily on the pupae and adults.

Midges emerge year-round. Because of this you need to be prepared at all times during the season to find fish feeding on them. Close observation is paramount for recognizing midging fish. There is rarely anything unique about a riseform that would indicate midge feeding; the actual presence of midges on the water is the strongest clue. Just as important though is knowing when and where they are likely to be a factor.

For instance, on lakes, midges are always near the top of the list of items rising fish might be taking. Stillwaters are extremely rich with midges, which generally stimulate more rises of trout than any other insect. Conversely, the importance of midges on rivers varies with the season. During the summer months when so many other insects are hatching, midges are at the bottom of our list of likely foods. This doesn't mean that fish aren't feeding on them, it's just that experience tells us to go with midges only when all other insects have been ruled out. From late fall to early spring midges are usually the only aquatic insect emerging, and consequently top the list of foods of rising fish.

Whether on lakes or streams, midge emergences can occur at all times of the day. Midges emerge at the surface, and it is the pupal phase that trout usually concentrate on. On streams we fish our imitations dead drift, in the surface film. When fishing lakes we often slowly strip our pupae across the paths of cruising fish; this little bit of motion can make all the difference at times.

Midges are subject to many emergence defects, and cripples and stillborns are common. Fish feed readily on such flies and we always carry imitations with trailing shucks. These patterns are fished dry and since they can be seen they are easier to fish than pupal imitations. Fully emerged adults are not fed on by trout as frequently as the pupae are, and we don't usually fish their imitations.

How important midge larvae are is unclear. Several years ago the late Ross Merigold presented us with a midge larva he fished on the Madison called the Serendipity. This fly has since proven to be the most productive nymph to be fished on the Madison in years. It is, of course, pure speculation to suggest that the fish are taking the fly as a midge, but nonetheless the Serendipity is a remarkable fly. Perhaps there *is* more midge activity on the Madison in the summer than previously thought.

Midges have provided us with some memorable fishing over the years, and an episode of several years ago comes immediately to mind. We had arrived at McAtee Bridge on the Madison River about one o'clock in the afternoon with strict instructions to be back in town by four-thirty for a New Year's Eve celebration. Winter fishing is always chancy, and in typical Montana fashion there was a brisk wind blowing at the bridge. Otherwise things seemed tolerable, and we did notice a number of adult midges assembling into mating clumps along shore.

Eventually, some of these clumps of adults drifted into the currents and we saw the odd fish beginning to rise. As the fish rose so did the wind, from brisk to gale force. But, we decided that since we had driven all the way down we should try our luck. We had been denied too many times before in the winter, and we weren't going down without a fight. We strung up and headed out, deciding to fish together so we could suffer together.

Conditions got worse as we hit the river, which is typical for our winter jaunts. Snow began falling horizontally, and the wind chill got serious. We lasted twenty minutes before our neoprenes froze, our gloves froze, our reels froze and our rod guides froze. Yes, we lost again, but not before catching the last fish of the year (*one* last fish).

It was a white out on the drive back until we hit Pine Butte, where miraculously the storm began clearing. At Slide Inn it was sunny and calm.   Though the storm gripped the mountains on all sides, it was actually pleasant as we checked along Sifton's wall for fish. Sure enough, a couple of fish were eating midges. Could we get rigged before the storm set in again? Hadn't we had enough?

We agreed we had had enough, that there would be plenty of other chances, and that it was, after all, New Year's Eve. But what the heck, we were there, and what fisherman could leave rising fish?

Mayflies

Species	April	May	June	July	August	September	October
Baetis tricaudatus	10 ———————————————————————						31
Baetis punctiventris		1 ———————————————————					31
Rhithrogena		25 —————————————————				5	
Pale Morning Dun		10 —————————————————				5	
Green Drake			15 ——————— 31		25 ———	15	
Brown Drake			20 ——————— 31				
Flav			10 ———————————— 10				
Gray Drake				1 ———————————		15	
Callibaetis			15 —————————————————			15	
Tricorythodes			25 —————————————————			15	
Pink Lady					1 ——— 4		
Attenella margarita					18 ———————————		4
Serratella tibialis					20 ———————————		5
Mahogany Dun					20 ——— 30		
Heptagenia					15 ———————————		1

91

Caddisflies

Species	April	May	June	July	August	September	October
Brachycentrus	10 ——————————————			4 25 ——	30		
Hydropsyche		15 ———————————————————————————					16
Helicopsyche		28 ————————		10			
Glossosoma		31 —————————————————————				21	
Oecetis			10 ——	5			
Cheumatopsyche			15 —————————		5		
Lepidostoma			15 ——————————————————			4	
Arctopsyche			20 ——	25			
Hesperophylax				15 ——	5		
Rhyacophila				1 ————	30		
Micrasema				15 ——	8		
Mystacides				20 ————	30		

Other Insects

Species	April	May	June	July	August	September	October
Salmonfly		20 ——————		30			
Golden Stone			25 ——————		31		
Little Yellow Stone				1 ———	15		
Damselflies				1 ———	30		
Midges			Year-round				

Fly Patterns

There are many, many patterns that will work as imitations of the various hatches we've covered; the following are merely our favorites. We have listed recipes for patterns that may not be widely known.

Mayflies
Baetis tricaudatus
1. Pheasant Tail Nymph
2. *Baetis* Emerger
Hook: Tiemco 5210 or 100, #l8 - #24.
Thread: 8/0 gray.
Tail: Woodduck flank fibers.
Body: Grayish-olive dubbing.
Hackle: Two turns of a Mallard duck shoulder or snipe feather.
3. Sparkle Dun
Hook: Tiemco 5210 or 100, #l8 - #24.
Thread: 8/0 gray.
Tail (shuck): Olive/brown zelon, one-half to a full hook shank in length.
Body: Grayish-olive dubbing.
Wing: Natural deer hair.

All Sparkle Duns are tied in the same style; the differences are in size, body color, and occasionally shuck color. We will list just these ingredients in future patterns.
4. Biplane
Hook: Tiemco 5210 or 100, #l8 - #24.
Thread: 8/0 olive.
Tail (shuck): Olive/brown zelon.
Body: Grayish-olive dubbing.
Wing: Gray zelon tied spent.
Baetis punctiventris
1. Sparkle Dun
Tiemco 100, #22 - #24, bright green body, olive shuck.

2. Sparkle Spinner
>   Hook: Tiemco l00, #22 - #24.
>   Thread: 8/0, color to match body.
>   Tail: Dun hackle fibers.
>   Body: Bright green or tan dubbing.
>   Wing: White zelon tied spent, half spent, or upright.

As with the Sparkle Dun, we will list only size and body color on future patterns.

Rhithrogena

1. *Rhithrogena* Emerger
>   Hook: Tiemco 5210 or l00, #14 - #16.
>   Thread: 8/0 olive.
>   Tails: Gray partridge fibers.
>   Body: Pale olive dubbing.
>   Hackle: Mottled gray partridge, two or three turns, trimmed on bottom. This pattern can be fished wet or dressed and fished dry.

2. Sparkle Dun
>   Tiemco 5210 or l00, #14 - #16, pale olive body, brown shuck.

3. Sparkle Spinner
>   Tiemco 5210 or l00, #14 - #16, olive/brown body.

Pale Morning Dun

1. Pheasant Tail Nymph

2. Pale Morning Dun Nymph
>   Hook: Tiemco 5210 or l00, #16 - #18.
>   Thread: 8/0 brown.
>   Tail: Brown partridge fibers.
>   Body: Brown rabbit, mixed with yellow antron.
>   Thorax: Brown rabbit.
>   Wingcase: Gray polycelon.

3. Pale Morning Dun Emerger
>   Hook: Tiemco 5210 or l00, #16-#18.
>   Thread: 8/0 yellow.
>   Tail (shuck): Brown zelon.
>   Body: Yellowish dubbing.
>   Wing case: Light gray polycelon.
>   Hackle: Two turns of starling hackle.

4. Pale Morning Dun Sparkle Dun

Tiemco 5210 or 100, #16 - #18, yellowish body, brown zelon shuck.

5. Sparkle Spinner

Tiemco 5210 or l00, #l6 -#18, pale olive or rusty body.

Green Drake

1. Green Drake Emerger

Hook: Tiemco 52l2, #l0-#l4.

Thread: 8/0 olive or yellow.

Tail: Moose body hair.

Body: Olive dubbing.

Rib: Yellow polyester thread.

Hackle: Grizzly dyed yellowish-olive.

Brown Drake

1. Brown Drake Nymph

Hook: Tiemco 52l2, #8-#l2

Thread: 8/0 brown.

Tails: Four ringneck pheasant tail fibers.

Body: Light brown dubbing.

Gills: Gray pheasant aftershaft feather tied on at tail and wound forward the length of the abdomen.

Rib: Brown polyester thread.

Wing case: Gray polycelon.

Thorax: Light hare's ear dubbing picked out.

An emerger pattern may be tied similarly by replacing the tails with tan zelon and enlarging the wingcase. This emerger pattern should be fished on the surface.

2. Brown Drake Parachute

Hook: Tiemco l00, #10 - #12.

Thread: 3/0 brown monocord.

Tail: Moose body hair.

Body: Light brown dubbing.

Ribbing: 3/0 brown monocord.

Wing: Natural deer hair.

Hackle: Grizzly dyed amber, parachute style.

3. Brown Drake Spinner

Hook: Tiemco 52l2, #10 - #12.
Thread: 8/0 brown.
Tails: Three moose hairs.
Body: Light brown dubbing.
Rib: Brown polyester thread.
Wing: Tan zelon or grizzly and brown hackle mixed and trimmed top and bottom.

Flav

1. Sparkle Dun

Tiemco 5210 or l00, #l4 - #l6, olive body, brown zelon shuck.

2. Sparkle Spinner

Tiemco 5210 or l00, #l4 - #l6, pale olive or rusty body.

Gray Drake

1. Gray Drake Spinner

Hook: Tiemco 5210 or 100, #l0 - #l4.
Thread: 8/0 gray.
Tail: Dun hackle fibers.
Body: Tan dubbing.
Rib: Brown polyester thread.

Wing: Dun hackle wound and clipped on top. A strip of gray polycelon is then pulled over the top and tied off at the head. This aids flotation on large spinner patterns. A wing of light dun zelon tied spent may also be used.

Callibaetis

1. *Callibaetis* Nymph

Hook: Tiemco l00, #l4 - #l6.
Thread: 8/0 tan.
Tails: Gray partridge fibers.
Body: Tan dubbing.
Wingcase: Gray polycelon.
Thorax: Same as body, picked out.

2. Sparkle Dun

Tiemco 5210 or l00, #14 - #16, tan body, pale gray shuck.

3. Sparkle Spinner
Tiemco 5210 or l00, #14 - #l6, tan body.

Tricorythodes
1. Sparkle Dun
Tiemco l00, #20 - #24, black or olive body, brown shuck.

2. Sparkle Spinner
Tiemco l00, #20 - #24, black body.

Pink Lady
1. Pink Lady Soft Hackle
Hook: Tiemco l00, #l4 - #16.
Thread: 8/0 gray.
Tail: Gray partridge hackle fibers.
Body: Pinkish olive dubbing.
Hackle: Pale dun hen hackle, two turns.

2. Sparkle Dun
Tiemco 5210 or l00, #l4 - #l6, pinkish olive body, light brown shuck.

Attenella margarita
1. Fur Nymph
Hook: Tiemco 5210, #l8.
Thread: 8/0 brown.
Tail: Brown partridge fibers.
Body: Dark brown dubbing.
Thorax: Same as body, picked out slightly.

2. Peacock
Tiemco 5210, #18. Just wrap peacock on the hook and trim a taper from front to back.

3. Pheasant Tail Nymph
4. Sparkle Dun
Tiemco 5210, #l8, olive body, brown shuck.

5. Sparkle Spinner
Tiemco 5210, #l8, olive or rusty body.

Serratella tibialis
  1. Fur Nymph
      Hook: Tiemco 5210 or 100, #16 - #18.
      Thread: 8/0 brown.
      Tails: Brown partridge fibers.
      Body: Dark brown dubbing.
      Thorax: Same as body, slightly picked out.
  2. Pheasant Tail Nymph
  3. Sparkle Dun
      Tiemco 5210, #16 - #18, olive/brown body, brown
          shuck.
  4. Sparkle Spinner
      Tiemco 5210, #18, brown body.
Mahogany Dun
  1. Fur Nymph
      Hook: Tiemco 5210, #16.
      Thread: 8/0 brown.
      Tail: Brown partridge fibers.
      Body: Brown dubbing.
      Wingcase (optional): Gray polycelon.
      Thorax: Same as body, slightly picked out.
  2. Sparkle Dun
      Tiemco 5210, #16, brown body, brown shuck.
Heptagenia
  1. Sparkle Dun
      Tiemco 5210 or 100, #14- #16, grayish brown body,
          light brown shuck.

Caddisflies
Brachycentrus
  1. Antron Caddis Pupa
      Hook: Tiemco 5210 or 100, #14 - #16.
      Thread: 8/0 gray or black.
      Shuck: Amber zelon, tied very short.
      Body: Olive antron dubbing, loop dubbed.
      Legs: Brown partridge hackle fibers.
      Head: Dark gray dubbing.
This caddis pupa can be tied for most caddis species; we
will list only the appropriate sizes and body colors on
future flies.

2. Soft Hackle

    Tiemco 5210 or 100, #14 - #16, roughly dubbed olive body, several turns of Snipe or Jackdaw hackle.

3. X-Caddis

    Hook: Tiemco 5210 or l00, #l4 - #l6.

    Thread: 8/0 olive.

    Shuck: Amber zelon.

    Body: Olive antron dubbing.

    Wing: Natural deer hair.

The X-caddis is a good emerging caddis pattern for all caddis. The only variables are size and body color, and for future flies we will list just these features.

4. Hemingway Caddis, #14 - #16.

Hydropsyche

1. Antron Caddis Pupa

    Tiemco 5210 or l00, #l4 - #l6, brownish yellow body.

2. Iris Caddis

    Hook: Tiemco 5210 or 100, #l4 - #16.

    Thread: 8/0 brown.

    Shuck: Amber zelon.

    Body: Pale green or tan dubbing, loop dubbed.

    Wing: Gray or white zelon, looped and tied low over the body.

    Head: Tan dubbing, shaggy.

This is another excellent emerging caddis pattern. It should be dressed and fished dry. We will list body color and size variations for other species.

3. LaFontaine Sparkle Pupa, tan, #14 - #16.

4. X-Caddis

    Tiemco 5210 or 100, #14 - #16, pale green or tan body.

5. Elk Hair Caddis, #14 - #16.

Helicopsyche

1. Antron Caddis Pupa

    Tiemco l00, #20 - #22, amber body, dark gray head.

2. *Helicopsyche* **adult**
> Hook: Tiemco l00, #20 - #22.
> Thread: 8/0 black.
> Body: Amber dubbing.
> Wing: Dark natural deer hair.

Oecetis
1. *Oecetis* **Spent Caddis**
> Hook: Tiemco 5210 or l00, #l6 - #18.
> Thread: 8/0 brown.
> Body: Golden yellow or bright green dubbing.
> Wing: Natural deer hair tied sparse, followed by several turns of English woodcock hackle or brown partridge hackle, swept back.

Glossosoma
1. Antron Caddis Pupa
> Tiemco l00, #20 - #22, grayish black body.
2. X-Caddis
> Tiemco 100, #20 - #22, grayish black body.

Cheumatopsyche
1. Antron Caddis Pupa
> Tiemco 5210, #18, olive body.
2. LaFontaine Sparkle Pupa, olive, #18.
3. X-Caddis
> Tiemco 5210, #l8, olive body.
4. Paul's Caddis

Lepidostoma
1. Antron Caddis Pupa
> Tiemco 5210, #l8, olive/brown body.
2. X-Caddis
> Tiemco 5210, #l8, olive/brown body.
3. Elk Hair Caddis, #18.
4. Spent Caddis
> Hook: Tiemco 5210, #18.
> Thread: 8/0 tan.
> Body: Olive dubbing.
> Wing: Natural elk hair, tied sparse, in front of which is wrapped a brown partridge hackle. This hackle should be swept back and simulates the wings awash on the surface.

Arctopsyche
    1. *Arctopsyche* **larva**
        Hook: Tiemco 3761, #10.
        Thread: 8/0 brown.
        Body: Brownish olive or olive antron dubbing.
        Legs: Brown partridge hackle fibers
        Head: Dark brown dubbing.
    2. *Arctopsyche* **adult**
        Hook: Tiemco 5210 or 100, #10 - #12.
        Thread: 8/0 brown.
        Body: Olive antron dubbing.
        Wing: Natural brown deer hair.
        Hackle: Brown or grizzly dyed brown.
    3. Brown Elk Hair Caddis, #8 - #10.
Hesperophylax
    1. Elk Hair Caddis, #8 - #12.
    2. Kaufmann's Stimulator, olive, #12 - #14.
Rhyacophila
    1. *Rhyacophila* **larva**
        Hook: Tiemco 3761, #14 - #16.
        Thread: 8/0 black.
        Body: Bright green antron dubbing over a foundation of lead wire.
        Legs: Two turns of starling hackle.
        Head: Black dubbing.
    2. X-Caddis
        Tiemco 5210 or 100, #14 - #16, olive body.
    3. Henryville Caddis, #14 -#16.
Micrasema
    1. Antron Caddis Pupa
        Tiemco 5210, #18 - #20, green body.
    2. Iris Caddis
        Tiemco 5210, #18 - #20, green body, dark gray head.

3. *Micrasema* Spent Adult

Hook: Tiemco 5210, #18 - #20.
Thread: 8/0 black
Body: Green dubbing.
Wing: Sparse, dark natural deer hair, followed by two or three turns of starling hackle, swept back.

Mystacides

1. *Mystacides* adult

Hook: Tiemco 5210, #l6 - #18.
Thread: 8/0 black.
Body: Dark gray or amber antron dubbing.
Wing: Black or dark natural deer hair.

Stoneflies

Salmonfly

1. Salmonfly Nymph

Hook: Tiemco 300, #6 - #8.
Thread: 3/0 black.
Tail: Brown stripped goose fibers.
Body: Black/orange variegated chenille.
Hackle: Dark brown, four or five wraps openly spaced to hook eye.

2. Matt's Adult Stonefly

Hook: Mustad 94840, #6 - #8.
Thread: 3/0 orange monocord.
Body: Orange poly macrame cord.
Wing: Elk mane.
Collar: Deer hair.
Head: Spun deer hair clipped to shape.

4. Jughead

Golden Stone

1. Golden Stone Nymph

Hook: Tiemco 300, #6 - #8.
Thread: 3/0 yellow.
Tails: Brown stripped goose quills.
Body: Brown/yellow variegated chenille over lead wire.
Hackle: Brown, four or five wraps openly spaced to the hook eye.

2. Kaufmann's Golden Stone Nymph

3. Kaufmann's Stimulator, sizes #6 - #10.

Little Yellow Stone - Adult

Hook: Tiemco 5210 or 100, #12-#18.

Thread: 8/0 red.

Tag: Red tying thread.

Body: Bright yellow dubbing.

Wing: Yellow dyed deer or elk hair.

Hackle: Grizzly or ginger.

Damselflies

1. Henry's Lake Damsel

Hook: Tiemco 5212, #6 - #10.

Thread: 8/0 olive.

Tails: Tuft of green marabou fibers.

Body: Green dubbing, thin, or green wool yarn.

Thorax: Peacock herl.

Hackle: Brown, openly palmered over thorax.

2. Damsel Adult

Hook: Tiemco 100, #10 - #12.

Thread: 8/0 tan or white.

Body: Extended body of tan or blue foam.

Wings: Grizzly hackle tips or white zelon.

Hackle: Several turns of grizzly hackle.

Midges

1. Fur Pupa

Hook: Tiemco 100, #14 - #24.

Thread: 8/0 black.

Body: Black dubbing, thin, ribbed with gray thread.

Thorax: Black dubbing, picked out slightly.

2. Serendipity

Hook: Tiemco 2487, #14 - #22.

Thread: 8/0, color to match body.

Body: Zelon—red, brown, or olive.

Head: Tuft of natural deer hair, trimmed short.

3. Zelon Midge

Hook: Tiemco 100, #18 - #24.

Thread: 8/0 black.

Shuck: White or dun zelon.

Body: Black dubbing, thin, ribbed with gray thread.

Wing: White zelon, tied back over the body.

Head: Black dubbing.

4. Griffith's Gnat